WOODROW WILSON

PATRIOTISM THROUGH LITERATURE

THE
SPIRIT OF DEMOCRACY

Patrick Henry University Press
Colorado Springs, Colorado

The Spirit of Democracy

by
Lyman P. Powell
Gertrude W. Powell

ISBN: 1-58963-450-0

Copyright © 2001 by Fredonia Books

Reprinted from the 1918 edition

Patrick Henry University Press
An Imprint of Fredonia Books
Colorado Springs, Colorado
http://www.patrickhenryuniversitypress.com

All rights reserved, including the right to reproduce this book, or portions thereof, in any form.

In order to make original editions of historical works available to scholars at an economical price, this facsimile of the original edition of 1918 is reproduced from the best available copy and has been digitally enhanced to improve legibility, but the text remains unaltered to retain historical authenticity.

THE CONTENTS

		PAGE
THE PRESIDENT'S WAR MESSAGE	Woodrow Wilson	1
AMERICA	Samuel Francis Smith	5
CLARION	Harold T. Pulsifer	6
YE THAT HAVE FAITH	Owen Seaman	7
THE MEANING OF AMERICANISM	Charles Evans Hughes	8
A THANKSGIVING	Marion Couthouy Smith	10
AMERICA	Bayard Taylor	12
AMERICA ENTERS THE WAR	David Lloyd George	14
ARMAGEDDON	Sir Edwin Arnold	16
WHAT DID YOU SEE OUT THERE, MY LAD?	John Oxenham	18
AMERICA FIRST	Woodrow Wilson	20
THE NEW BANNER	Katrina Trask	26
A LITANY IN THE DESERT	Alice Corbin Henderson	27
VICTORY BEFORE PEACE	Albert Shaw	28
AMERICANS, HAIL!	Sir William Watson	30
COMRADES	Richard Hovey	33
WHY WE MUST WIN	Frank O. Lowden	34
I AM AN AMERICAN	Elias Lieberman	39
THE SEARCHLIGHTS	Alfred Noyes	40
THE UNITED STATES COMES OF AGE	Hamilton Holt	42
TO AMERICA	Charles Langbridge Morgan	43
THE REVEILLE	Bret Harte	44
OPPOSING PRINCIPLES	Talcott Williams	46
BOSTON HYMN	Ralph Waldo Emerson	47
DIES IRAE — DIES PACIS	John Oxenham	48
GOLDEN BOYS	Winifred M. Letts	49
WHY WE FIGHT	Theodore Roosevelt	50
THE RIDERLESS HORSE	Harold T. Pulsifer	51
A CAVALRY CATCH	William Sharp	52
A LULLABY	G. R. Glasgow	52

THE CONTENTS

	PAGE
OUR COMMON HERITAGE............*Arthur J. Balfour*	54
PEACE HYMN FOR ENGLAND AND AMERICA......... *George Huntington*	57
MALBROUK—ET NOUS........................	58
THE MEMORIAL DAY ADDRESS ....*Woodrow Wilson*	59
GETTYSBURG ADDRESS ....*Abraham Lincoln*	61
ABRAHAM LINCOLN WALKS AT MIDNIGHT....... *Vachel Lindsay*	62
UNION.................... *Virginia Fraser Boyle*	63
SUPPORTING THE GOVERNMENT..............*Elihu Root*	66
"BREATHES THERE THE MAN"....... *Sir Walter Scott*	71
"OF OLD SAT FREEDOM ON THE HEIGHTS"........ *Alfred Tennyson*	72
THE PRESENT CRISIS..........*James Russell Lowell*	73
CARRY ON!..................... *Robert W. Service*	74
CHANGES AHEAD.................*Marion LeRoy Burton*	76
HYMN OF FREEDOM...............*Mary Perry King*	79
PATRIOTISM............................*Lyman Abbott*	80
EARTH CALLS TO HEAVEN..*William Pierson Merrill*	81
THE LITTLE STAR IN THE WINDOW............. *John Jerome Rooney*	82
THE BATTLE BETWEEN RIGHT AND MIGHT............. *Frank O. Lowden*	85
FROM "ODE OF DEDICATION" ....*Hermann Hagedorn*	90
"OVER THERE"...................*Harvey M. Watts*	91
TO THE AMERICAN PEOPLE.......... *Bayard Taylor*	91
THE EDUCATION WE ARE FIGHTING FOR..*Henry Van Dyke*	93
A HYMN................. ....*Robert Grant*	95
THE RETURN......................*John Freeman*	97
FIGHTING BATTLES WITH SPEECH AND PEN............. *Charles Evans Hughes*	98
GIVE US MEN....................*Bishop of Exeter*	102
BE STRONG.............*Maltbie Davenport Babcock*	103

THE CONTENTS

		PAGE
THE MEN AT THE FRONT	David Lloyd George	104
THE CONNAUGHT RANGERS	Winifred M. Letts	105
"BADDEST BOY"		106
FLAG-DAY ADDRESS	Woodrow Wilson	108
THE STAR-SPANGLED BANNER	Francis Scott Key	110
MAKERS OF THE FLAG	Franklin K. Lane	112
THE FLAG	Edith M. Thomas	114
FOLLOW THE FLAG	Theodore Marburg	115
THE KID HAS GONE TO THE COLORS	William Herschell	117
PUTTING THE FLAG ON THE FIRING LINE	Theodore Roosevelt	119
FAME'S TRUE APPLAUSE	George Edward Woodberry	121
STAND BY THE FLAG		122
THE CALL TO BATTLE	Gilbert Sheldon	122
THE WORLD SIGNIFICANCE OF THE WAR	William H. Taft	124
TOGETHER	Alfred Austin	126
PEACE	Elizabeth Barrett Browning	127
THE CALL OF THE REPUBLIC	George Haven Putnam	128
THE BUILDING OF THE SHIP	Henry Wadsworth Longfellow	129
"IT IS TIME"	Lloyd Roberts	130
A SIMPLE SONG FOR AMERICA	Karle Wilson Baker	130
OUR MORAL LEADERSHIP	Edmund J. James	132
"OH MOTHER OF A MIGHTY RACE"	William Cullen Bryant	134
ON PATROL		136
ENGLAND UNSHEATHES THE SWORD	Herbert H. Asquith	138
THE CALL	R. E. Vernède	140
AN INVOCATION	Beatrice Barry	142
THE SPIRES OF OXFORD	Winifred M. Letts	143
TO THE ARMY!	King Albert	144
THE PRAYER	Amelia Josephine Burr	145
IN FLANDERS FIELDS	John McCrae	147

THE CONTENTS

	PAGE
BELGIUM SHALL RISE............*Cardinal Mercier*	148
TO BELGIUM ....*Eden Phillpotts*	151
LIÈGE............. ....*Sir William Watson*	152
LA BRABANÇONNE............*Florence Attenborough*	153
THE FIGHTERS OF FRANCE.............*Anatole France*	154
THE MARSEILLAISE...............*Rouget de Lisle*	156
YOUR LAD, AND MY LAD.........*Randall Parrish*	157
LILLE, LAON, AND ST. DIÉ....... ...*John H. Finley*	159
VIVIANI AT SPRINGFIELD...........	162
THE FATHERLAND.............*James Russell Lowell*	165
THE BLUE AND THE GRAY IN FRANCE.*George M. Mayo*	165
A WELCOME TO MARSHALL JOFFRE..*Charles S. Whitman*	166
THE NIGHTINGALES OF FLANDERS .*Grace H. Conkling*	168
SOMEWHERE IN FRANCE...... ....*Harvey M. Watts*	169
THE CHILDREN OF FRANCE........... *Marshal Joffre*	170
THE VICTOR OF THE MARNE.....................	
....*Robert Underwood Johnson*	170
GRAND-PÈRE... . . ..*Robert W. Service*	171
CHILDREN OF FRANCE...... .....*Gertrude Robinson*	172
FRATERNAL MESSAGE TO AMERICA ..*Gabriele d'Annunzio*	174
ON THE ITALIAN FRONT........*George E. Woodberry*	175
DECLARATION OF WAR BY ITALY.*Gabriele d'Annunzio*	175
OUT OF ROME... ....*Clinton Scollard*	176
TO THE YOUNG MEN OF ITALY...*Giuseppe Mazzini*	177
SERBIA'S SACRIFICE. . . ..*Major Stobart*	180
SERBIA.. . . .. *Amelia Josephine Burr*	181
SCARRED...............	182
SALONIKA IN NOVEMBER................*Brian Hill*	182
WOMAN'S DUTY ....*Mrs. Percy V. Pennybacker*	184
THE BRAVE AT HOME ....*Thomas B. Read*	186
TO WOMAN.................*Lawrence Binyon*	187
MOTHERING...... ...... *H. Buchanan Ryley*	187
TO A MOTHER ....*Eden Phillpotts*	188
ANY WOMAN TO A SOLDIER...*Grace Ellery Channing*	189

THE CONTENTS

		PAGE
LABOR MUST BEAR ITS PART	*Woodrow Wilson*	191
THE KEEPERS OF THE LIGHT	*Theodosia Garrison*	194
A SONG OF SERVICE	*Theodosia Garrison*	194
MORE THAN A NAME	*Samuel Gompers*	196
WHAT THE STATE IS	*Sir William Jones*	198
SOLDIERS OF FREEDOM	*Katharine Lee Bates*	199
THE KHAKI	*Henry Edward Warner*	200
LESSONS OF THE WAR	*Theodore Roosevelt*	201
AMERICA RESURGENT	*Wendell Phillip Stafford*	202
IN FORTY WEST		203
SOLDIERS ALL	*Daniel M. Henderson*	204
COMRADES IN A COMMON CAUSE	*Bishop Brent*	206
BRITONS AND GUESTS	*Edith M. Thomas*	207
CHRIST IN FLANDERS	*A British Soldier*	208
ONWARD, CHRISTIAN SOLDIERS	*S. Baring-Gould*	209
ENGLAND'S CASE	*Herbert H. Asquith*	211
CANADA TO ENGLAND	*Wilfred Campbell*	211
AUSTRALIA TO ENGLAND	*Archibald T. Strong*	213
INDIA TO ENGLAND	*Nizamat Jung*	214
A MESSAGE TO IRELAND	*Florence Goff*	215
GOING HOME	*Robert W. Service*	216
CANADA STANDS FAST	*Sir Robert Laird Borden*	218
TO CANADA	*Katharine Lee Bates*	219
A CRY FROM THE CANADIAN HILLS	*Lilian Leveridge*	221
THE RECKONING	*Theodore G. Roberts*	223
A LEAGUE OF NATIONS	*Woodrow Wilson*	225
A PRAYER IN TIME OF WAR	*Alfred Noyes*	226
AMERICA TO FRANCE AND GREAT BRITAIN	*Harold T. Pulsifer*	227
THE CHALLENGE	*H. T. Suddrith*	229
THE HOLY QUEST	*Rabbi Stephen S. Wise*	230
HANDS ALL ROUND	*Alfred Tennyson*	232
CARRY ON!	*John Oxenham*	233

THE CONTENTS

	PAGE
TO THE UNITED STATES OF AMERICA..*Robert Bridges*	234
THE WESTERN LAND ....*Caroline Hazard*	234
A MESSAGE TO AMERICA...............*Romain Rolland*	236
AMERICA THE BEAUTIFUL........*Katharine Lee Bates*	237
WE SHALL REMEMBER THEM....*James Terry White*	239
KEEP THE ROAD OF DEMOCRACY OPEN..*William E. Borah*	240
RESURREXIT..................*Grace Ellery Channing*	243
THE ROAD TO FRANCE........*Daniel M. Henderson*	244
THE GUARDS CAME THROUGH.........*Conan Doyle*	245
WORLD RECONSTRUCTION ....*Oscar S. Straus*	248
JUDGMENT DAY.....................*John Oxenham*	249
THE UNIVERSAL PEACE............*Alfred Tennyson*	249
THE YEAR BEFORE US..............*John Timothy Stone*	251
LORD, GIVE ME A PLACE.........................	253
GOD SAVE OUR SPLENDID MEN........	253
THE RED CROSS....................*Woodrow Wilson*	255
BEHIND THE GUNS............*Henry Edward Warner*	259
THE RED CROSS SPIRIT SPEAKS .....*John H. Finley*	260
GREY KNITTING....................*Katherine Hale*	261
THE TASK OF THE RED CROSS........*Newton D. Baker*	263
YOUTH SPEAKS TO YOUTH.......................	264
THE RED CROSS NURSES........*Thomas L. Masson*	265
WITH THE AMERICAN RED CROSS IN FRACE	
....................*Henry P. Davison*	267
THE FEET OF THE CHILDREN........*Nora A. Smith*	269
WHEN THE BOYS COME HOME......... .....*John Hay*	271

A LIST OF THE PORTRAITS

	FACING PAGE
Woodrow Wilson	Frontispiece
Charles Evans Hughes	8
David Lloyd George	14
Albert Shaw	28
Frank O. Lowden	34
Hamilton Holt	42
Talcott Williams	46
Theodore Roosevelt	50
Arthur James Balfour	54
Elihu Root	66
Marion LeRoy Burton	76
Lyman Abbott	80
Franklin K. Lane	112
William Howard Taft	124
George H. Putnam	128
Edmund J. James	132
King Albert	144
Cardinal Mercier	148
M. Anatole France	154
Rene Raphael Viviani	162
Charles S. Whitman	166
Marshal Joffre	170
Gabriele D'Annunzio	174
Major St. Clair Stobart	180
Samuel Gompers	196
Bishop Brent	206
Sir Robert Laird Borden	218
Rabbi Stephen S. Wise	230
Romain Rolland	236
Oscar S. Straus	248
John Timothy Stone	251
Newton D. Baker	263

ACKNOWLEDGMENTS

The compilers of this volume extend their grateful acknowledgments to the following authors and publishers for permission to use copyrighted selections:

Harold T. Pulsifer, of *The Outlook*, for "Clarion" and "The Riderless Horse," published by the Houghton Mifflin Company.

Marion Couthouy Smith for "A Thanksgiving."

Doran & Co. for John Oxenham's "What Did You See Out There, My Lad," "Dies Irae—Dies Pacis," and "Carry On"; Amelia Josephine Burr's "The Prayer," and the selection from Major Stobart's *Flaming Sword in Serbia and Elsewhere*.

Katrina Trask for "The New Banner."

Mrs. Alice Corbin Henderson and *The Yale Review* for "A Litany in the Desert"; *The Yale Review* for Winifred M. Letts' "The Connaught Rangers."

Albert Shaw for his editorial in the *Review of Reviews*, "Victory before Peace."

Small, Maynard & Company for Richard Hovey's "Comrades."

Elias Lieberman and the Cornhill Company for "I Am an American."

Frederick A. Stokes & Co. for Alfred Noyes' "The Searchlights" and "A Prayer in Time of War."

The Macmillan Company for Vachel Lindsay's "Abraham Lincoln Walks at Midnight," from *The Congo and Other Poems*; Archibald T. Strong's "Australia to England," and Eden Phillpotts' "To Belgium."

E. P. Dutton & Co. for Winifred M. Letts' "Golden Boys" and "The Spires of Oxford, from *The Spires of Oxford*."

Virginia Fraser Boyle for "Union."

Collier's Weekly for Mary Perry King's "Hymn of Freedom."

William Pierson Merrill for "Earth Calls to Heaven."

John Jerome Rooney for "The Little Star in the Window."

The Outlook for the stanza from Hermann Hagedorn's "Ode of Dedication," Daniel M. Henderson's "Soldiers All," and Harold T. Pulsifer's "America to France and Great Britain."

Harvey M. Watts for "Over There" and "Somewhere in France."

Robert Grant for "A Hymn," which appeared in *Scribner's Magazine*.

Edith M. Thomas for "The Flag."

William Herschell for "The Kid Has Gone to the Colors," copyright by The Bobbs-Merrill Company, Indianapolis.

ACKNOWLEDGMENTS

Theodore Marburg for "Follow the Flag."

George E. Woodberry for "Fame's True Applause" and "On the Italian Front."

Lloyd Roberts for the stanza from "Come Quietly, Britain."

Karle Wilson Baker for "A Simple Song for America."

The *New York Times* for Beatrice Barry's "Invocation" and Edith M. Thomas' "Britons and Guests."

Randall Parrish for "Your Lad, and My Lad."

John H. Finley for "Lille, Laon, and St. Dié."

Grace Hazard Conkling and *Everybody's Magazine* for "The Nightingales of Flanders."

Thomas L. Masson, editor of *Life*, for his "Red Cross Nurses," which appeared in the *Red Cross Magazine*, and Gertrude Robinson's "The Children of France," published in *Life*.

Clinton Scollard for "Out of Rome."

John Lane Company for the selection from Emile Cammaerts' "King and Emperor."

Amelia Josephine Burr and *Everybody's Magazine* for "Serbia."

The Living Church for Lieutenant Ryley's "Mothering," which recently appeared in its columns.

Grace Ellery Channing for "Any Woman to a Soldier," which appeared in the *Saturday Evening Post*, and "Resurrexit," which appeared in the Boston *Transcript*.

McClure's Magazine for Theodosia Garrison's "Keepers of the Light" and "A Song of Service."

Katharine Lee Bates for "America the Beautiful," published by Thomas Y. Crowell and Co., and "Soldiers of Freedom," which appeared in *Good Housekeeping*.

Wendell Phillip Stafford and the Washington *Evening Star* for "America Resurgent."

Fleming H. Revell for Wilfred Campbell's "Canada to England."

Caroline Hazard for "The Western Land."

The National Arts Club for Daniel M. Henderson's "The Road to France."

Henry Edward Warner and the Richmond *Times Dispatch* for "Behind the Guns."

Nora Archibald Smith for "The Feet of the Children," which appeared in *The Outlook*.

Katherine Hale for "Grey Knitting."

"Going Home," "Grand-père," and "Carry On" are from *Rhymes of a Red Cross Man*, published by Barse & Hopkins, New York.

The selections from John Hay, Bret Harte and Laurence Binyon are used by permission of and by special arrangement with the Houghton Mifflin Company, Boston.

THE PREFACE

The war at last is calling forth prose and poetry to match its cosmic character. Our President's addresses easily average higher taken as a group than any others made on either side of the ocean in intellectual comprehensiveness, moral elevation, restrained feeling, and that rhythmic quality which one detects in some of Lincoln's greater speeches.

But many other addresses are close seconds to our President's. Never in any previous national or world crisis have so many speakers risen to the dignity of the occasion. Even truer is this of verse, and more poems which promise to live have perhaps been written since the war began than in any other period so brief of human history.

The Spirit of Democracy—unlike other books—aims to assemble in convenient arrangement, for school purposes, many of the most stirring speeches and most virile poems applicable to the present situation. In preparation of this book we have hoped to render it easier for busy teachers to avoid the more conventional readings and declamations, and instead to give their pupils the prose and verse certain to make them more loyal and intelligent patriots.

The speeches of the war have been open to the entire world, but those brought together in this volume are believed to represent the great cause with special fitness.

As to the verse, after the consideration of much of the bewildering variety that has appeared, we have included in this volume poems which will, it is hoped, reflect all of the various considerations involved.

L. P. P.
G. W. P.

The American's Creed

"*I BELIEVE in the United States of America as a government of the people, by the people, for the people, whose just powers are derived from the consent of the governed; a democracy in a republic; a sovereign Nation of many sovereign States; a perfect Union, one and inseparable, established upon those principles of freedom, equality, justice, and humanity for which American patriots sacrificed their lives and fortunes.*

"*I therefore believe it is my duty to my country to love it; to support its Constitution; to obey its laws; to respect its flag; and to defend it against all enemies.*"

THE SPIRIT OF DEMOCRACY

THE PRESIDENT'S WAR MESSAGE[1]
WOODROW WILSON

Gentlemen of the Congress:

I have called the Congress into extraordinary session because there are serious, very serious, choices of policy to be made, and made immediately, which it was neither right nor constitutionally permissible that I should assume the responsibility of making.

On the third of February last I officially laid before you the extraordinary announcement of the Imperial German Government that on and after the first day of February it was its purpose to put aside all restraints of law or of humanity and use its submarines to sink every vessel that sought to approach either the ports of Great Britain and Ireland or the western coasts of Europe or any of the ports controlled by the enemies of Germany within the Mediterranean.

That had seemed to be the object of the German submarine warfare earlier in the war, but since April of last year the Imperial Government had somewhat restrained the commanders of its undersea craft in conformity with its promise then given to us that passenger boats should

[1] From the speech delivered April 2, 1917.

not be sunk and that due warning would be given to all other vessels which its submarines might seek to destroy when no resistance was offered or escape attempted, and care taken that their crews were given at least a fair chance to save their lives in their open boats.

The new policy has swept every restriction aside. Vessels of every kind, whatever their flag, their character, their cargo, their destination, their errand, have been ruthlessly sent to the bottom without warning and without thought of help or mercy for those on board, the vessels of friendly neutrals along with those of belligerents.

When I addressed the Congress on the 26th of February last I thought it would suffice to assert our neutral rights with arms, our right to use the seas against unlawful interference, our right to keep our people safe against unlawful violence. But armed neutrality, it now appears, is impracticable. Because submarines are in effect outlaws, when used as the German submarines have been used against merchant shipping, it is impossible to defend ships against their attacks, as the law of nations has assumed that merchantmen would defend themselves against privateers or cruisers, visible craft giving chase upon the open sea. It is common prudence in such circumstances, grim necessity indeed, to endeavor to destroy them before they have shown their own intention. They must be dealt with upon sight, if dealt with at all.

With a profound sense of the solemn and even tragical character of the step I am taking and of the grave responsibilities which it involves, but in unhesitating obedience to what I deem my constitutional duty, I advise that the Congress declare the recent course of the Imperial German

Government to be in fact nothing less than war against the Government and people of the United States, that it formally accept the status of belligerent which has thus been thrust upon it and that it take immediate steps not only to put the country in a more thorough state of defense, but also to exert all its power and employ all its resources to bring the Government of the German Empire to terms and end the war.

The world must be made safe for democracy. Its peace must be planted upon the tested foundations of political liberty. We have no selfish ends to serve. We desire no conquests, no dominion. We seek no indemnities for ourselves, no material compensation for the sacrifices we shall freely make. We are but one of the champions of the rights of mankind. We shall be satisfied when those rights have been made as secure as the faith and the freedom of nations can make them.

Just because we fight without rancor and without selfish object, seeking nothing for ourselves but what we shall wish to share with all free people, we shall, I feel confident, conduct our operations as belligerents without passion and ourselves observe with proud punctilio the principles of right and of fair play we profess to be fighting for.

It will be all the easier for us to conduct ourselves as belligerents in a high spirit of right and fairness because we act without animus, not in enmity toward a people or with the desire to bring any injury or disadvantage upon them, but only in armed opposition to an irresponsible government which has thrown aside all considerations of humanity and of right and is running amuck.

We have no quarrel with the German people. We have no feeling toward them but one of sympathy and friendship. It was not upon their impulse that their government acted in entering the war. It was not with their previous knowledge or approval. It was a war determined upon as wars used to be determined upon in the old unhappy days, when peoples were nowhere consulted by their rulers and wars were provoked and waged in the interest of dynasties or of little groups of ambitious men who were accustomed to use their fellow men as pawns and tools.

It is a distressing and oppressive duty, gentlemen of the Congress, which I have performed in thus addressing you. There are, it may be, many months of fiery trial and sacrifice ahead of us. It is a fearful thing to lead this great, peaceful people into war, into the most terrible and disastrous of all wars, civilization itself seeming to be in the balance.

But the right is more precious than peace, and we shall fight for the things which we have always carried nearest our hearts—for democracy, for the right of those who submit to authority to have a voice in their own Governments, for the rights and liberties of small nations, for a universal dominion of right by such a concert of free people as shall bring peace and safety to all nations and make the world itself at last free.

To such a task we can dedicate our lives and our fortunes, everything that we are and everything that we have, with the pride of those who know that the day has come when America is privileged to spend her blood and her might for the principles that gave her birth and happiness and the peace which she has treasured.

God helping her, she can do no other.

AMERICA
SAMUEL FRANCIS SMITH

My country, 't is of thee,
Sweet land of liberty,
　Of thee I sing;
Land where my fathers died,
Land of the Pilgrims' pride,
From every mountain side
　Let freedom ring.

My native country, thee,
Land of the noble free,
　Thy name I love;
I love thy rocks and rills,
Thy woods and templed hills;
My heart with rapture thrills
　Like that above.

Let music swell the breeze,
And ring from all the trees
　Sweet Freedom's song;
Let mortal tongues awake,
Let all that breathe partake,
Let rocks their silence break,
　The sound prolong.

Our fathers' God, to Thee,
Author of liberty,
　To Thee we sing;
Long may our land be bright
With Freedom's holy light;
Protect us by Thy might,
　Great God, our King.

CLARION

HAROLD T. PULSIFER

God send a prophet tongued with flame
To sear the Nation's self-content;
Lest writ in words of livid shame
Ye read, *eternal banishment*.

Dread banishment from those High Halls
Your fathers builded wide and deep.
Once, twice, and thrice the trumpet calls,
How long shall ye lie bound in sleep?

The skies are dark with homing ghosts:
With Belgian blood the world is red:
Through the salt sea in piteous hosts
Still troop the phantoms of your dead!

Shrill-voiced your chosen leaders cry
The need of freedom for your gold.
Thank God the men at Concord lie
Too deep to know what ye have sold.

Was it for this the ancient hand
Carved out the riches of your soil?
Then let the sea blot out the land,
The storm blot out the wasted toil!

Blot out the dream of Washington,
Blot out the vision Lincoln knew,
Blot out their hope of air and sun,
Bring back the night they overthrew!

Once, twice, and thrice the trumpet calls,—
The sword is nigh, the sword is come!
Awake, O watchmen on the walls,
And lift your dead hands to the drum!

YE THAT HAVE FAITH
OWEN SEAMAN

Ye that have faith to look with fearless eyes
Beyond the tragedy of a world at strife,
And know that out of death and night shall rise
The dawn of ampler life,

Rejoice, whatever anguish rend the heart,
That God has given you a priceless dower,
To live in these great times and have your part
In Freedom's crowning hour.

That ye may tell your sons who see the light
High in the heavens — their heritage to take —
"I saw the powers of Darkness put to flight;
I saw the morning break."

THE MEANING OF AMERICANISM[1]
CHARLES EVANS HUGHES

We want something more than thrills in our patriotism — we want thought; we want intelligence — a new birth of the sentiment of unity in the nation.

My dream of America is America represented in public office by its best men working entirely for the good of the Republic and according to the laws and ordinances established by the people for the government of their conduct and not for the personal or political desires and ambitions; America working her institutions as they were intended to be worked, with men whose sole object shall be to secure the end for which the offices were designed.

And if one will throw his personal fortunes to the winds, if he will perform in each place, high or low, the manifest obligation of that place, we will soon have those victories of democracy which will make the Fourth of July in its coming years a far finer and nobler day than it has ever been in the fortunate years of the past.

When we are thinking of the ideals of democracy, we are thinking of the schools, and we deplore every condition in which we find man lower than he should be under a free government, and we want greater victories of democracy that the level of success shall be raised.

We are not a rash people; we are not filled with the spirit of militarism. We are not anxious to get into trouble, but if anybody thinks that the spirit of service and sacrifice is lost and that we have not the old

---
[1] From the speech delivered at Easthampton L. I., July 4, 1916.

CHARLES EVANS HUGHES

sentiment of self-respect, he doesn't understand the United States.

We want patriotism, and I don't think that we are going to lose it very soon, although I do devoutly hope that out of the perils and difficulties of this time may come a new birth of the sentiment of unity. I do hope that in the midst of all these troublesome conditions we will have a better realization of our national strength and the import of our democratic institutions.

The boy is going to thrill at the sight of the flag to-day just as he did fifty years or one hundred years ago. We are all going to thrill when we hear the words of our national hymn, and we think of the long years of struggle and determination that have brought us to this hour. But we want something more than thrills in our patriotism; we want thought, we want intelligence.

Not vast extent of territory, not great population, not simply extraordinary statistics of national wealth, although they speak in eloquent words of energy and managing ability; but what we need more than anything else is an intelligent comprehension of the ideals of democracy. Those ideals are that every man shall have a fair and equal chance according to his talents. It is not an ideal of democracy that one alone shall emerge because of conspicuous ability, but that there shall be a great advance of the plain people of the country, upon whom the prosperity of the country depends.

Wherever the Stars and Stripes float there is a shrine.

It is all very well to talk about the Declaration of Independence and the strong sentiments it contains, but that was backed by men who couldn't have committed it to memory, men who couldn't have repeated it, but men in whose lives was the incarnation of independence and whose spirit was breathed into that immortal document.

It is because we had men who were willing to suffer, to die, to venture, to sacrifice, that we have a country, and it is only by that spirit that we will ever be able to keep a country. I love to think of those hardy men coming here with the same spirit that led the pioneers to the West and Farther West, the same spirit which in every part of our land has accounted for our development.

Quiet men, not noisy men; sensible men, not foolish men; straight men, honest men, dependable men, real men — that is what we mean by Americanism.

A THANKSGIVING
MARION COUTHOUY SMITH

Not for our harvest,
   Our fields' increase,
Not for our safety,
   Our vaunted peace,
Our word-clad justice,
   Our light-flung gift,
But for hearts that waken.
   For dreams that lift —
     We praise Thee, O God

For Belgium's sword
   That faltered never,
For the splendid woe
   Of her lost endeavour;
For the great free peoples

A THANKSGIVING

In grim advance,
For the might of England,
  The light of France—
    We praise Thee, O God!

For Italy's flower
  Of fearless youth;
For nations waking
  From dream to truth;
For the flame of Serbia
  That mounts in death,
The fire that fails not
  With blood and breath—
    We praise Thee, O God!

For dull ease broken
  By sharpest dole,
For the dart that is driven
  Through flesh to soul;
For wrath made sterner
  By right's eclipse,
For brave songs breaking
  From pain-wrung lips—
    We praise Thee, O God!

For faith that is born
  From the burning nest,
For the spirit's flight
  On its starward quest,
For peace that dwells
  At the heart of strife,
For death that scatters
  The seed of life—
    We praise Thee, O God!

AMERICA[1]

BAYARD TAYLOR

Foreseen in the vision of sages,
    Foretold when martyrs bled,
She was born of the longing of ages,
    By the truth of the noble dead
    And the faith of the living fed!
No blood in her lightest veins
Frets at remembered chains,
Nor shame of bondage has bowed her head.
    In her form and features still
    The unblenching Puritan will,
    Cavalier honor, Huguenot grace,
    The Quaker truth and sweetness,
And the strength of the danger-girdled race
Of Holland, blend in a proud completeness.
From the homes of all, where her being began
    She took what she gave to Man;
    Justice, that knew no station,
        Belief, as soul decreed,
    Free air for aspiration,
Free force for independent deed!
    She takes, but to give again,
As the sea returns the rivers in rain;
And gathers the chosen of her seed
From the hunted of every crown and creed.
    Her Germany dwells by a gentler Rhine;
    Her Ireland sees the old sunburst shine;
    Her France pursues some dream divine;
    Her Norway keeps his mountain pine;

---

[1] From "The National Ode."

Her Italy waits by the western brine;
    And broad-based under all,
Is planted England's oaken-hearted mood,
As rich in fortitude
As e'er went worldward from the island-wall!
    Fused in her candid light,
To one strong race all races here unite:
Tongues melt in hers, hereditary foemen
Forget their sword and slogan, kith and clan:
    'T was glory, once, to be a Roman:
She makes it glory, now, to be a man!

AMERICA ENTERS THE WAR[1]
DAVID LLOYD GEORGE

I am the last man in the world, knowing for three years what our difficulties have been, what our anxieties have been, and what our fears have been — I am the last man in the world to say that the succor which is given from America is not in itself something to rejoice at, and to rejoice at greatly. But I also say that I value more the knowledge that America is going to win a right to be at the conference table when the terms of peace are discussed.

That conference will settle the destiny of nations and the course of human life for God knows how many years. It would have been a tragedy, a tragedy for mankind, if America had not been there, and there with all her influence and her power.

I can see peace, not a peace to be a beginning of war, not a peace which will be an endless preparation for strife and bloodshed, but a real peace. The world is an old world. You have never had the racking wars that have rolled like an ocean over Europe.

Europe has always lived under the menace of the sword. When this war began, two thirds of Europe was under autocratic rule. Now it is the other way about, and democracy means peace. The democracy of France hesitated; the democracy of Italy hesitated long before it entered; the democracy of this country sprang back with a shudder and would never have entered that caldron had it not been for the invasion of Belgium; and if

---
[1] From a speech delivered before the American Luncheon Club of London, April 12, 1917.

David Lloyd George

Prussia had been a democracy, there would have been no war.

Many strange things have happened in this war, aye, and stranger things will come, and they are coming rapidly. There are times in history when this world spins so leisurely along its destined course that it seems for centuries to be at a standstill. There are awful times when it rushes along at giddying pace, covering the track of centuries in a year. Those are the times we are living in now.

To-day we are waging one of the most devastating wars that the world has ever seen. To-morrow, to-morrow, not perhaps distant to-morrows, war may be abolished forever from the category of human crimes. This may be something like that fierce outburst of winter which we now are witnessing before we complete the time for the summer.

It is written of those gallant men who won that victory on Monday, from Canada, from Australia, and from this old country—it has proved that in spite of its age it is not decrepit—it is written of those gallant men that they attacked at dawn. Fitting work for the dawn—to drive out of forty miles of French soil those miscreants who had defiled her freedom. They attacked with the dawn. It is a significant phrase.

The great nations represented in the struggle for freedom—they are the heralds of dawn. They attacked with dawn, and those men are marching forward in the full radiance of that dawn, and will emerge into the full light of a perfect day.

ARMAGEDDON

SIR EDWIN ARNOLD

Marching down to Armageddon—
　Brothers, stout and strong!
Let us cheer the way we tread on
　With a soldiers' song!
Faint we by the weary road,
　Or fall we in the rout,
Dirge or Pæan, Death or Triumph!—
　Let the song ring out!

We are they who scorn the scorners—
　Love the lovers—hate
None within the world's four corners—
　All must share one fate;
We are they whose common banner
　Bears no badge or sign,
Save the Light which dyes it white—
　The Hope that makes it shine.

We are they whose bugle rings,
　That all the wars may cease;
We are they will pay the Kings
　Their cruel price for Peace;
We are they whose steadfast watchword
　Is what Christ did teach,—
"Each man for his Brother first—
　And Heaven, then, for each."

We are they who will not falter—
　Many swords or few—
Till we make this Earth the altar

ARMAGEDDON

Of a worship new;
We are they who will not take
    From palace, priest, or code,
A meaner Law than "Brotherhood"—
    A lower Lord than GOD.

Marching down to Armageddon—
    Brothers, stout and strong!
Ask not why the way we tread on
    Is so rough and long!
God will tell us when our spirits
    Grow to grasp His plan!
Let us do our part to-day—
    And help Him, helping Man!

Shall we even curse the madness,
    Which for "ends of State"
Dooms us to the long, long sadness
    Of this human hate?
Let us slay in perfect pity
    Those that must not live;
Vanquish, and forgive our foes—
    Or fall—and still forgive!

We are those whose unpaid legions,
    In free ranks arrayed,
Massacred in many regions—
    Never once were stayed:
We are they whose torn battalions,
    Trained to bleed, not fly,
Make our agonies a triumph,—
    Conquer, while we die!

Therefore, down to Armageddon —
  Brothers, bold and strong —
Cheer the glorious way we tread on
  With this soldier's song!
Let the armies of the old Flags
  March in silent dread!
Death and Life are one to us,
  Who fight for Quick and Dead!

WHAT DID YOU SEE OUT THERE, MY LAD?

JOHN OXENHAM

What did you see out there, my lad,
  That has set that look in your eyes?
You went out a boy, you have come back a man,
With strange new depths underneath your tan;
What was it you saw out there, my lad,
  That set such deeps in your eyes?

"Strange things — and sad — and wonderful —
  Things that I scarce can tell —
I have been in the sweep of the Reaper's scythe —
  With God — and Christ — and hell.

"I have seen Christ doing Christly deeds;
  I have seen the Devil at play;
I have grimped to the sod in the hand of God;
  I have seen the Godless pray.

"I have seen Death blast out suddenly
  From a clear blue summer sky;

WHAT DID YOU SEE OUT THERE, MY LAD?

I have slain like Cain with a blazing brain,
   I have heard the wounded cry.

"I have lain among the dead,
   With no hope but to die;
I have seen them killing the wounded ones,
   I have seen them crucify.

"I have seen the Devil in petticoats
   Wiling the souls of men;
I have seen great sinners do great deeds,
   And turn to their sins again.

"I have sped through hells of fiery hail,
   With fell red-fury shod;
I have heard the whisper of a voice,
   I have looked in the face of God."

You've a right to your deep, high look, my lad,
   You have met God in the ways;
And no man looks into His face
   But he feels it all his days.
You've a right to your deep, high look, my lad,
   And we thank Him for His grace.

AMERICA FIRST[1]
WOODROW WILSON

There is a very great thrill to be had from the memories of the American Revolution, but the American Revolution was a beginning, not a consummation, and the duty laid upon us by that beginning is the duty of bringing the things then begun to a noble triumph of completion. For it seems to me that the peculiarity of patriotism in America is that it is not a mere sentiment. It is an active principle of conduct. It is something that was born into the world, not to please it but to regenerate it. It is something that was born into the world to replace systems that had preceded it and to bring men out upon a new plane of privilege. The glory of the men whose memories you honor and perpetuate is that they saw this vision, and it was a vision of the future. It was a vision of great days to come when a little handful of three million people upon the borders of a single sea should have become a great multitude of free men and women spreading across a great continent, dominating the shores of two oceans, and sending West as well as East the influences of individual freedom. These things were consciously in their minds as they framed the great government which was born out of the American Revolution; and every time we gather to perpetuate their memories it is incumbent upon us that we should be worthy of recalling them and that we should endeavor by every means in our power to emulate their example.

[1] From a speech delivered at Washington, D. C., before the Daughters of the American Revolution, October 11, 1915.

The American Revolution was the birth of a nation; it was the creation of a great free republic based upon traditions of personal liberty which theretofore had been confined to a single little island, but which it was purposed should spread to all mankind. And the singular fascination of American history is that it has been a process of constant re-creation, of making over again in each generation the thing which was conceived at first. You know how peculiarly necessary that has been in our case, because America has not grown by the mere multiplication of the original stock. It is easy to preserve tradition with continuity of blood; it is easy in a single family to remember the origins of the race and the purposes of its organization; but it is not so easy when that race is constantly being renewed and augmented from other sources, from stocks that did not carry or originate the same principles.

So from generation to generation strangers have had to be indoctrinated with the principles of the American family, and the wonder and the beauty of it all has been that the infection has been so generously easy. For the principles of liberty are united with the principles of hope. Every individual, as well as every nation, wishes to realize the best thing that is in him, the best thing that can be conceived out of the materials of which his spirit is constructed. It has happened in a way that fascinates the imagination that we have not only been augmented by additions from outside, but that we have been greatly stimulated by those additions. Living in the easy prosperity of a free people, knowing that the sun had always been free to shine upon us and prosper our undertakings, we did not realize how hard the task of liberty is and how rare the privilege of liberty is; but men were drawn out of every climate and out of every race because of an irresistible attraction of their spirits to the American ideal. They thought of America as lifting, like that great statue in the harbor of New York, a torch to light the pathway of men to the things that they desire, and men of all sorts and conditions struggled toward that light and came to our shores with an eager desire to realize it, and a hunger for it such as some of us no longer felt, for we were as if satiated and satisfied and were indulging ourselves after a fashion that did not belong to the ascetic devotion of the early devotees of those great principles. Strangers came to remind us of what we had promised ourselves and through ourselves had promised mankind. All men came to us and said, "Where is the bread of life with which you promised to feed us, and have you partaken of it yourselves?" For my part, I believe that the constant renewal of this people out of foreign stocks has been a constant source of reminder to this people of what the inducement was that was offered to men who would come and be of our number.

Now we have come to a time of special stress and test. There never was a time when we needed more clearly to conserve the principles of our own patriotism than this present time. Every political action, every social action, should have for its object in America at this time to challenge the spirit of America; to ask that every man and woman who thinks first of America should rally to the standards of our life.

America has a great cause which is not confined to the American continent. It is the cause of humanity itself. I do not mean in anything that I say even to imply a judgment upon any nation or upon any policy, for my object here this afternoon is not to sit in judgment upon anybody but ourselves and to challenge you to assist all of us who are trying to make America more than ever conscious of her own principles and her own duty. I look forward to the necessity in every political agitation in the years which are immediately at hand of calling upon every man to declare himself, where he stands. Is it America first or is it not?

We ought to be very careful about some of the impressions that we are forming just now. There is too general an impression, I fear, that very large numbers of our fellow-citizens born in other lands have not entertained with sufficient intensity and affection the American ideal. But the number of such is, I am sure, not large. Those who would seek to represent them are very vocal, but they are not very influential. Some of the best stuff of America has come out of foreign lands, and some of the best stuff in America is in the men who are naturalized citizens of the United States. I would not be afraid upon the test of "America first" to take a census of all the foreign-born citizens of the United States, for I know that the vast majority of them came here because they believed in America; and their belief in America has made them better citizens. They can say that they have bought this privilege with a great price. They have left their homes, they have left their kindred, they have broken all the nearest and dearest ties of human life in order to come to a new land, take a new rootage, begin a new life, and so by self-sacrifice express their confidence in a new principle; whereas, it cost us none of these things. We were born into this privilege; we were rocked and cradled in it; we did nothing to create it; and it is, therefore, the greater duty on our part to do a great deal to enhance it and preserve it. I am not deceived as to the balance of opinion among the foreign-born citizens of the United States, but I am in a hurry for an opportunity to have a line-up and let the men who are thinking first of other countries stand on one side and all those that are for America first, last, and all the time stand on the other side.

Now, you can do a great deal in this direction. When I was a college officer I used to be very much opposed to hazing; not because hazing is not wholesome, but because sophomores are poor judges. I remember a very dear friend of mine, a professor of ethics on the other side of the water, was asked if he thought it was ever justifiable to tell a lie. He said Yes, he thought it was sometimes justifiable to lie; "but," he said, "it is so difficult to judge of the justification that I usually tell the truth." I think that ought to be the motto of the sophomore. There are freshmen who need to be hazed, but the need is to be judged by such nice tests that a sophomore is hardly old enough to determine them. But the world can determine them. We are not freshmen at college, but we are constantly hazed. I would a great deal rather be obliged to draw pepper up my nose than to observe the hostile glances of my neighbors. I would a great deal rather be beaten than ostracized. I would a great deal rather endure any sort of physical hardship if I might have the affection of my fellow-men. We constantly discipline our fellow-citizens by having an opinion about them. That is the sort of discipline we ought now to administer to everybody who is not to the very core of his heart an American.

Just have an opinion about him and let him experience the atmospheric effects of that opinion!

It has seemed to me that my privilege this afternoon was not merely a privilege of courtesy, but the real privilege of reminding you—for I am sure I am doing nothing more—of the great principles which we stand associated to promote. I for my part rejoice that we belong to a country in which the whole business of government is so difficult. We do not take orders from anybody; it is a universal communication of conviction, the most subtle, delicate, and difficult of processes. There is not a single individual's opinion that is not of some consequence in making up the grand total, and to be in this great coöperative effort is the most stimulating thing in the world. A man standing alone may well doubt his own judgment. He may mistrust his own intellectual processes; he may even wonder if his own heart leads him right in matters of public conduct; but if he finds his heart part of the great throb of national life, there can be no doubt about it. If that is his circumstance, then he may know that he is part of one of the great forces of the world.

I would not feel any exhilaration in belonging to America if I did not feel that she was something more than a rich and powerful nation. I should not feel proud to be in some respects and for a little while her spokesman if I did not believe that there was something else than physical force behind her. I believe that the glory of America is that she is a great spiritual conception and that in the spirit of her institutions dwells not only her distinction but her power. The one thing that the world cannot permanently resist is the moral force of great and triumphant convictions.

THE NEW BANNER
KATRINA TRASK

O fellow-citizens of storm-tossed Lands,
  War weary! Sound the bugle-note! Arise!
New steadfast standards wait your eager hands,
  The Star of Promise orbs to meet your eyes.
      Great Kings must pass, that mankind may be free
      Beneath the banner of Democracy!

The Mighty Ruler of this mortal life
  Has wisdom, not by mortals understood:
The seeds of blood, the deeds of wanton strife
  Shall some day harvest unexpected good.
      Great Kings shall pass and every nation be
      Ruled by the people — for the people, free.

When the mad anguish of this stricken world —
  Where valiant heroes daily fight and fall —
Has passed and Freedom's banners are unfurled,
  Then shall we know the reason for it all!
      Then every waiting, heart-sick land shall see
      The ultimate design of Destiny!

Brave men and women, laboring in toil —
  Who, faithful, fight with willing sword or pen,
Who work to break the rock or till the soil —
  Shall wear the high insignia of men.
      All Kings must pass, that every man may be
      A monarch in his manhood, strong and free!

Beyond the present, unimagined woe,
  A glorious Day is breaking o'er the earth:
As Spring flowers blossom, after ice-bound snow,
  The God of Gods shall bring new things to birth.
      It is the dawn! Great forces are set free!
      All Hail the Day! World-wide Democracy!

A LITANY IN THE DESERT
ALICE CORBIN HENDERSON

I

On the other side of the Sangre de Cristo mountains there is a great welter of steel and flame. I have read that it is so   I know nothing of it here.

On the other side of the water there is terrible carnage. I have read that it is so. I know nothing of it here.

I do not know why men fight and die. I do not know why men sweat and slave. I know nothing of it here.

II

Out of the peace of your great valleys, America, out of the depth and silence of your deep canyons,

Out of the wide stretch of yellow corn-fields, out of the stealthy sweep of your rich prairies,

Out of the high mountain peaks, out of the intense purity of your snows,

Invigorate us, O America.

Out of the deep peace of your breast, out of the sure strength of your loins,

Recreate us, O America.

Not from the smoke and the fever and fret, not from the welter of furnaces, from the fierce melting-pots of cities;

But from the quiet fields, from the little places, from the dark lamp-lit nights—from the plains, from the cabins, from the little house in the mountains,

Breathe strength upon us:

And give us the young men who will make us great.

VICTORY BEFORE PEACE
ALBERT SHAW

The United States has joined a powerful league of nations whose object is to enforce peace. It is reasonable to hope that the end of the war is nearer in consequence. Whether or not the existing war is to be shortened by our assumption of the status of belligerency, it is fairly certain that our own future peace as well as that of all other leading nations, for a hundred years to come, is much less likely to be disturbed. We have gone into this war to make the rule of reason respected, and to make the peace dream of ages a working reality of the early future.

If a peace could have been made last winter it was conceivable that the main ends of justice might have been met and durable solutions adopted. But the continuance and development of the war has made it necessary that victory should precede peace. The cause of the Anglo-French group of allies has become clarified in the movement of events, until now that cause is identical with the best interests of mankind. America had hoped to join a future league to enforce peace after war was ended. But events have shown that we could expect no such League of the Future, unless we were prepared to play a larger part in the League of the Present.

When great crises arise and decisions of historic moment are made, it is usually true that there has been a long series of historic events and situations more or less obscure leading inevitably to the startling climax. No nation in Europe desired in 1914 to become involved in war. Yet the fuel had been piling up for the great conflagration

Copyright by Underwood & Underwood

ALBERT SHAW

for many years; and it was written in the book of fate that a torch should be applied in the Balkans that would set the whole world aflame.

We in the United States, looking on at these developments, were conscious of great fears and also of great hopes. There was room in the world for the industry and commerce of Germany, as well as for the efforts of England, France, and Japan. There was valuable and beneficent progress visible in all the leading countries. There was growing friendship across boundary lines among men of business, men of science, representatives of the labor movements, and exponents of arts and letters. It was ridiculous to say that the pursuits of peace had made the nations effeminate, or lacking in the so-called martial virtues. On the contrary, the disciplines of modern life, along with the applications of science, had given us a larger proportion of people sound in mind and body than at any other time in human history. Yet with all the fine progress of nations, the secret diplomacy of their dynasties and their foreign offices and the competitive extension of their political empires were in constant danger of bringing about either a succession of wars or one stupendous conflict. Over against the fears of war due to false policies, were the hopes based upon the growing common sense of mankind, upon steps taken in the Hague Conferences, upon arbitration treaties, and especially upon the constant growth of democratic influence and labor solidarity.

When the great war broke out, in 1914, we declared that it was fundamentally due to the fact that peoples were the victims of governments. We took the ground that if Germany had been as progressive in the creation of a truly representative government as she had been progressive in many other aspects of her national life and character, the war could not have occurred.

It is very annoying to the government-controlled press of Germany that President Wilson should have had the audacity in his address to Congress to make a sharp distinction between the German people and the Prussian autocracy that now constitutes the government of the Empire. Yet this distinction is not merely invidious or theoretical. According to President Wilson, one of our objects in taking part in the war against the German Government is to secure the emancipation and true welfare of the German people. His address to Congress breathes no spirit of hatred. Having failed in his efforts a few months earlier to persuade the nations of Europe to negotiate a "peace without victory," it became evident to him that the war must go on until one side or the other had gained a marked degree of military success.

Thus the moral effect of having America committed to the common cause could hardly be overestimated.

—From *The Review of Reviews*, May, 1917

AMERICANS, HAIL!
SIR WILLIAM WATSON

Here, too, is greatness; here are heads grown gray
In council, not yet dreaming of repose;
Here are the athletes of debate, and here
The brains that are the lamps without whose light
Armies would grope and stumble, and noblest prowess
With a waste splendor dazzle a fruitless field.

AMERICANS, HAIL!

Here, also, his hot thirst for toil unslaked,
The sinews of his lithe mind unrelaxed,
Is he, our Empire's leader: he who set
The wheels of the machinery of victory
Whirring and spinning throughout all this isle,
Till Britain hummed as one great mill of war;
A man, no wraith or shadow; a live man,
Loathed by the specters and the counterfeits;
A man as human as your Lincoln was,
Not muffled up in formula and phrase,
With palisaded spirit, but giving us
Access and entrance to his hopes and fears,
And in companionship of glorious hazard
Bearing us with him, while he treads a road
Built like a causeway across flaming Hell;
Himself a flame of ardor and resolve,
Beset by all the tempests, but unquenched,
Being used to blasts, and native to the storm,
And thriving on the thunder from his prime.

Ours were the shame, if having such a leader
We proved unworthy at last to be so led,
And lowered the flag of an unshaken will,
And stooped our soul to a stature and a posture
Like theirs who preach a base truck with the foe.

*   *   *   *   *

With hope that can not wholly vanquish fear,
The veiled, unknown, tremendous morrow; we
With our own chiefs of camp and council; you
With yours; and at your head the famed, the trusted,
The hated and revered one: he whose speech
Is hazeless sister unto cloudless thought:

Who, flooding with a bland light all his theme,
Can, when the hour craves gallant archery,
Unquiver none the less a deadly lightning:
A mind 'twixt wariness and boldness poised,
Wide-watching and far-scouting, subtle and sage;
Cool as a pine at its firm heart is cool,
Tho secretly a colleague of the sun,
And living by his fire: a soul erect
E'en as the pine itself is; and altho
Towering amid the forest of your life
O'er all beside, still of that forest, still
One only of a hundred million trees
Knowing no difference in their right to Summer.

Ah, once, in the dead yesterday that seems
Entombed so deep, haply we did him wrong!
We knew not all; now, now we understand.
We are men, and see the man: large, patient, calm;
Freed from the trammels and the coils that bound
And half obscured him: standing there to-day,
Etched with no vagueness against no blurred sky:
Yonder concerting and controlling all
The instruments in that vast orchestra,
Your nation, whence there rises goldenly
Tho sternly, with far surge and tidal swell,
Not without sad and wailful underflow,
But mighty in heave and sound, all dissonance hushed
That new Heroic Symphony of war;
Heard throughout Earth with a grave thankfulness
By such as love great music; and perhaps
E'en on an ear divine not wholly lost,
Not utterly unacceptable to Heaven.

COMRADES
RICHARD HOVEY

Comrades, gird your swords to-night,
For the battle is with dawn!
Oh, the clash of shields together,
With the triumph coming on!
Greet the foe,
And lay him low,
When strong men fight together!

Comrades, watch the tides to-night,
For the sailing is with dawn!
Oh, to face the spray together,
With the tempest coming on!
Greet the sea
With a shout of glee,
When strong men roam together!

Comrades, give a cheer to-night,
For the dying is with dawn!
Oh, to meet the stars together,
With the silence coming on!
Greet the end
As a friend a friend,
When strong men die together!

—From *Songs from Vagabondia*

WHY WE MUST WIN
FRANK O. LOWDEN

This is not a mere war for territory. If it were, some point of common agreement might be reached. It is not a war sought as a balm to a Nation's wounded pride. If it were, that pride would have been swallowed up long ago in the horrors of the war. It is a war of ideas. And it is a war of two such big ideas that the world itself is not big enough to hold them both. One idea recognizes that, as Government is composed of the people, so Government is subject to the same moral tests, the same ethical obligations as the people who compose it. The idea for which the Central Empires contend is that the State is above all morality, all obligation to humanity, and that its only consideration is, what is best for itself.

At last we know the issue which we have to meet. The Prussian autocracy, a half century ago, declared that the law of force was the only law governing nations. The world heard, but did not heed the sinister threat. Now we know that this was no mere idle, academic utterance of the class-room. The idea, inspired by the history of the Hohenzollerns and given utterance by the State-controlled universities of the Empire, has flourished until it holds securely within its grip a great and powerful nation. Moved by this idea Germany has, with infinite patience, and ingenuity, and genius, built the greatest fighting machine the world has ever known.

That idea has grown until it has almost the force of a religious cult. It is spreading like a black cloud over the earth, and nothing will drive away that cloud but the

Frank O. Lowden

absolute triumph of our armies in this war. I believe from the bottom of my heart that the German people will gain more from their own decisive defeat than we will gain ourselves. We are at war, not with any people, but with this idea which, if we do not fight it to the death, will dominate and rule and ruin the earth. Why should not they invade Belgium? It was to their military advantage, and in their new philosophy, advantage to the State is all that counts. Why isn't a treaty a scrap of paper, if their philosophy is sound? Why should not they sink unarmed merchant ships and deliberately drown men and women and children, if that would help them to impose their new Kultur upon the world? Why should we be surprised at their dropping bombs upon hospitals where wounded and dying men lie? These men had dared to fight for that other idea, the outworn idea that there is such a thing as the honor of nations. The German war cult has been consistent — diabolically consistent — throughout. It can answer every charge that has been made or may be made against it by an appeal to its basic idea that the nation is above the moral law — that national honor is but a phrase invented by the weaker nations to escape the power of the sword. Force, brute force, material force, force that can be seen and felt, and force alone, if they are right, should rule the world. Literature, music, the arts, and all the things of the spirit that make life sweet and beautiful are of use only if they prepare the people for war, and then, when war comes, serve to feed its flames.

The idea that moral considerations, considerations of justice, of humanity, of honor, bind the individuals of a State but not the State itself. is so monstrous that it threatens the civilization of the world. Yea, it will destroy even the civilization of the State itself, which holds to this idea. It corrupts its own citizens. The people of no country can have high ideals if their nation openly professes low ones. The conduct of Count von Bernstorff, the late German ambassador to this country, is a case in point. He followed faithfully the German idea. He was the honored guest of our Nation; the hospitality of our people and the freedom of our land were his. Professing daily his friendship for America, and though we were at peace with his country, he plotted destruction of railroads and munition plants, he fomented internal disorder, he filled our land with spies — but he was true to the principles of his master. And no man can serve a state which denies the existence of national honor, and not himself lose his own honor. Count von Bernstorff doubtless despised himself for the life of lies he lived amongst us. But he was loyal to the teachings of his country. When will men learn that there cannot be one set of ethics for men and another for nations? The idea that a nation can do no wrong, and that the moral considerations which bind individuals do not control in the activities of the State, must be stamped out for evermore if peace in any permanent form is ever to return to the world. Whatever is wrong when done by the individuals composing a nation, is equally wrong when done by the nation itself. The idea that it is a crime for one man to steal his neighbor's horse, but an heroic thing when seventy-five million, in the name of the State, steal a neighboring province, must be done to death. You cannot multiply vice by a number large enough to make vice a virtue.

Under the spell of this evil ideal they have forgotten all the splendid literature of their past; they have neglected the noble lines of Lessing, Goethe and Schiller, and have decorated that poet who has written "The Hymn of Hate." This ideal has seized their Science, and their scientists tell you to-day that they are but acting in accordance with the law of the survival of the fittest — that it is best for the world that weak nations and weak peoples be exterminated. That is the idea with which we are at war.

Oh, my friends, this idea which they let loose half a century ago, if it shall go on another half century will take the world back to the law of the jungle, and that cruel law will hold the world in its grip.

It is so hard to realize that such a danger can exist at this period of the world. Upon the whole we have made progress during the century and a half since we, as a nation, came into existence, and we assume that it must continue indefinitely; but that is not the history of the world. You will recall that away back, even before the time of the Christian Era, there was a splendid civilization in Greece, and that the Roman Republic had started upon its career of glory; but remember that all this civilization went out into the blackness of night and for centuries, in the Middle Ages, a sable pall covered the globe. Civilization has been beaten before, and it has taken centuries for it to emerge, and so again, with this threat, like a black cloud over every land, there never was so heavy a burden placed upon our patriotism as now — never in all our past.

This is not like any other war in which we were ever engaged. We had our great Civil War, the greatest war in the history of the world down to that time. But the present war means infinitely more to everyone of us than did the Civil War, and I will tell you why. If we, of the North, had lost in the Civil War, we still would have had some kind of a country. It would have been fragmentary and inglorious, perhaps, but we still would have had a home. There would have been some soil, above which our flag waved, and upon which we could dwell. But if this war in which we are engaged is lost, we will not even have the remnant of a country left, because the principle of absolutism will rest upon all the world. We not only will have no place which we can call our home, but there won't be a nook or a cranny in all the universe, where a lover of liberty can find refuge; because when this war is over, the world, all the world, will be altogether free, or altogether slave.

I do not know which is the more interested in this war, capital or labor, but I do know that nothing matters to either if we do not win the war. And capital cannot alone win the war, and labor cannot alone win the war. Therefore, it is time, as it never was before, for capital and labor to get together, to gather about the same board, to sit in the same council, and to resolve to merge all differences until their common danger shall be repelled.

America has been called the melting-pot of the nations. There are some evidences of late that the pot has grown cool and that it has failed in its work. Maybe the flames of this world-wide war were needed to make it red hot again. At any rate, we may hope that when the war is over there will come from that pot, only gold and dross, nd that our citizenship, whether native or foreign born will stand forth in but two classes,— genuine, war-tried Americans on the one hand. and dross on the other.

I AM AN AMERICAN
ELIAS LIEBERMAN

I am an American.
My father belongs to the Sons of the Revolution;
My mother, to the Colonial Dames.
One of my ancestors pitched tea overboard in Boston
    Harbor;
Another stood his ground with Warren;
Another hungered with Washington at Valley Forge.
My forefathers were America in the making:
They spoke in her council halls;
They died on her battle-fields;
They commanded her ships;
They cleared her forests.
Dawns reddened and paled.
Stanch hearts of mine beat fast at each new star
In the nation's flag.
Keen eyes of mine foresaw her greater glory:
The sweep of her seas,
The plenty of her plains,
The man-hives in her billion-wired cities.
Every drop of blood in me holds a heritage of patriotism.
I am proud of my past.
I am an American.

I am an American.
My father was an atom of dust,
My mother a straw in the wind,
To his serene majesty.
One of my ancestors died in the mines of Siberia;
Another was crippled for life by twenty blows of the *knut;*

Another was killed defending his home during the
    massacres.
The history of my ancestors is a trail of blood
To the palace-gate of the Great White Czar.
But then the dream came —
The dream of America.
In the light of the Liberty torch
The atom of dust became a man
And the straw in the wind became a woman
For the first time.
"See," said my father, pointing to the flag that fluttered
    near,
"That flag of stars and stripes is yours;
It is the emblem of the promised land.
It means, my son, the hope of humanity.
Live for it — die for it!"
Under the open sky of my new country I swore to do so;
And every drop of blood in me will keep that vow.
I am proud of my future.
I am an American.

THE SEARCHLIGHTS
ALFRED NOYES

Shadow by shadow, stripped for fight,
    The lean black cruisers search the sea.
Night-long their level shafts of light
    Revolve, and find no enemy.
Only they know each leaping wave
May hide the lightning, and their grave.

And in the land they guard so well
    Is there no silent watch to keep?

THE SEARCHLIGHTS

An age is dying, and the bell
   Rings midnight on a vaster deep.
But over all its waves, once more,
The searchlights move, from shore to shore.

And captains that we thought were dead,
   And dreamers that we thought were dumb,
And voices that we thought were fled,
   Arise, and call us, and we come;
And "Search in thine own soul," they cry;
   "For there, too, lurks thine enemy."

Search for the foe in thine own soul,
   The sloth, the intellectual pride,
The trivial jest that veils the goal
   For which our fathers lived and died:
The lawless dreams, the cynic Art,
That rend thy nobler self apart.

Not far, not far into the night
   These level swords of light can pierce;
Yet for her faith does England fight,
   Her faith in this our universe,
Believing Truth and Justice draw
From founts of everlasting law;

Therefore a Power above the State,
   The unconquerable Power returns.
The fire, the fire that made her great
   Once more upon her altar burns.
Once more, redeemed and healed and whole,
She moves to the Eternal Goal.

  This poem was called forth by General von Bernharde's statement that "Political morality differs from individual morality because there is no power above the State."

THE UNITED STATES COMES OF AGE
HAMILTON HOLT

The United States has come of age. For nearly a century and a half it has been growing up. It passed safely through the common ailments of childhood. It has suffered the disconcerting mysteries of adolescence. It has been racked by "growing pains." An almost mortal illness, safely weathered, left it stronger than before. It has put on bone and sinew and good solid flesh. It has grown in wisdom and stature.

Now, in God's good time, it has come to its majority. It has stepped out to take its place among its fellows on the earth. It has become a citizen of the world.

This is the deep and stirring significance of the President's address. The United States at a stroke assumes the rôle of a Great Power. It steps out of the Western Hemisphere into the world. It accepts its full share of responsibility for the world's peace and good order. It declares its right and duty and purpose to fight for justice, not only in the New World, but in the Old.

All this was implied in what we have already done. But it needed such a detailed and unequivocal statement to drive it home. Events have moved rapidly for us in the past year. It is no wonder that Europe has not realized how far we had come. It is no wonder that we ourselves were hardly conscious where we had arrived.

We are pledged to fight to the end to readjust the map of Europe. Our terms of peace include a free Poland, a return of Italia Irredenta, the freedom of Turkey's oppressed peoples, the redress of the crime of 1871 in Alsace-Lorraine, autonomy for parts of Austria-Hungary.

HAMILTON HOLT

A strange undertaking for the American people. An astounding breaking with the past. But in the world we have lived in for three years now it hardly seems strange. The past is more shadowy than it has ever been before. Our eyes are on the future.

The future beckons the American nation to a mighty responsibility. The nation goes forward with a bound.

—From *The Independent*, January 19, 1918.

TO AMERICA
CHARLES LANGBRIDGE MORGAN

When the fire sinks in the grate, and night has bent
Close wings about the room, and winter stands
Hard-eyed before the window, when the hands
Have turned the book's last page and friends are sleeping,
Thought, as it were an old stringed instrument
Drawn to remembered music, oft does set
The lips moving in prayer, for us fresh keeping
Knowledge of springtime and the violet.

And, as the eyes grow dim with many years,
The spirit runs more swiftly than the feet,
Perceives its comfort, knows that it will meet
God at the end of troubles, that the dreary
Last reaches of old age lead beyond tears
To happy youth unending. There is peace
In homeward waters, where at last the weary
Shall find rebirth, and their long struggle cease.

So, at this hour, when the Old World lies sick,
Beyond the pain, the agony of breath

Hard drawn, beyond the menaces of death,
O'er graves and years leans out the eager spirit.
First must the ancient die; then shall be quick
New fires within us. Brother, we shall make
Incredible discoveries and inherit
The fruits of hope, and love shall be awake.

THE REVEILLE
BRET HARTE

Hark! I hear the tramp of thousands,
  And of armed men the hum;
Lo! a nation's hosts have gathered
  Round the quick alarming drum, —
     Saying, "Come,
     Freemen, come!
Ere your heritage be wasted," said the quick alarming drum.

"Let me of my heart take counsel:
  War is not of life the sum.
Who shall stay and reap the harvest
  When the autumn days shall come?"
     But the drum
     Echoed, "Come!
Death shall reap the braver harvest," said the solemn-sounding drum.

"But when won the coming battle,
  What of profit springs therefrom?
What if conquest, subjugation,
  Even greater ills become?"

THE REVEILLE

    But the drum
    Answered, "Come!
You must do the sum to prove it," said the Yankee
    answering drum.

"What if, 'mid the cannon's thunder,
    Whistling shot and bursting bomb,
When my brothers fall around me,
    Should my heart grow cold and numb?"
    But the drum
    Answered, "Come!
Better there in death united, than in life a recreant,—
    Come!"

Thus they answered, — hoping, fearing,
    Some in faith, and doubting some,
Till a trumpet-voice, proclaiming,
    Said, "My chosen people, come!"
    Then the drum,
    Lo! was dumb,
For the great heart of the nation, throbbing, answered,
    "Lord, we come!"

OPPOSING PRINCIPLES[1]
TALCOTT WILLIAMS

We may as well understand that what we have long looked for, which through earth's mists men have seen as the coming of the dawn, the World State, is already here.

There is not a man in business who has not found himself affected by what has taken place. There is not a single man here or a single man between the oceans, who is not perfectly well aware that in a fashion he had never dreamed, in a manner he had never imagined, and which no statesman had predicted and no university had taught, there has suddenly dawned upon us all, that humanity is one, that all states are part of it, that we have ceased to look upon peoples, but instead we see humanity as a whole, and that every great act affects all humanity alike. Face to face with the World State, we need to be aware that what we are watching is not a war between nations any longer. It is civil war. It is a war between two great opposing principles of humanity; one looking to the organization of the State from above, and the other looking to its organization from below. One believing that authority can be conferred upon a few to exercise for the benefit of the many, and the other believing that nobody is wise enough to exercise authority in behalf of anyone else except by their choice and their consent.

It will be seven centuries next June since the cornerstone of the second of those principles was laid in the Great Charter signed by the barons and King John.

[1] Delivered before the Economic Club of Boston, February 8, 1915.

Photo by Brown Bros.

TALCOTT WILLIAMS

The great question is whether this principle shall widen, until it is recognized by all the world.

We cannot avoid it if we would, and we would not avoid it if we could. The great service which the United States can do towards obtaining peace is to continue to stand upon the protest which it uttered against the violation of the neutralization of one country until it has secured the acceptance, in the reorganization of the World State which is at hand, of this principle by the entire world.

This is the task which is before this country; this is the task which is slowly establishing itself before you; and there is not a single man here who does not believe that upon this principle and upon this principle alone the United States should endeavor to secure peace. Peace, when it comes, must begin a World State ruled either by militarism or by Republics; and in that great conflict, although victory may be delayed, although sacrifice may be required, here, in this city, with Concord and Bunker Hill at hand, no man can doubt as to the final and ultimate result.

BOSTON HYMN

RALPH WALDO EMERSON

The word of the Lord by night
To the watching Pilgrims came,
As they sat by the seaside,
And filled their hearts with flame.

God said, I am tired of kings,
I suffer them no more;
Up to my ear the morning brings
The outrage of the poor.

Think ye I made this ball
A field of havoc and war,
Where tyrants great and tyrants small
Might harry the weak and poor?

My angel—his name is Freedom—
Choose him to be your king;
He shall cut pathways east and west,
And fend you with his wing.

* * * * *

DIES IRAE — DIES PACIS
JOHN OXENHAM

"Only through Me!" . . . The clean, high call comes pealing,
Above the thunders of the battle-plain;—
"Only through Me can Life's red wounds find healing;
Only through Me shall earth find peace again.

Only through Me . . . Love's Might, all might transcending,
Alone can drain the poison-fangs of Hate.
Yours the beginning!—Mine a nobler ending,—
Peace upon Earth, and Man regenerate!

Only through Me can come the great awaking;
Wrong cannot right the wrongs that Wrong hath done;
Only through Me, all other gods forsaking,
Can ye attain the heights that must be won.

Only through Me shall Victory be sounded;
Only through Me can Right wield righteous sword;

Only through Me shall Peace be surely founded;
Only through Me! . . . Then bid Me to the Board!"

Can we not rise to such great height of glory?
Shall this vast sorrow spend itself in vain?
Shall future ages tell the woful story,—
"Christ by His own was crucified again"?

GOLDEN BOYS
WINIFRED M. LETTS

Not harps and palms for these, O God,
Nor endless rest within the courts of heaven—
These happy boys who left the football-field,
The hockey ground, the river, the eleven,
In a far grimmer game, with high-elated souls,
To score their goals.

Let these, O God, still test their manhood's **strength**,
Wrestle and leap and run,
Feel sea and wind and sun;
With Cherubim contend;
The timeless morning spend
In great celestial games.
Let there be laughter and a merry noise
Now that the fields of Heaven shine
With all these golden boys.

WHY WE FIGHT[1]
THEODORE ROOSEVELT

At the outbreak of the war our people were stunned, blinded, terrified by the extent of the world disaster. Those among our leaders who were greedy, those who were selfish and ease-loving, those who were timid and those who were merely short-sighted, all joined to blindfold the eyes and dull the conscience of the people so that it might neither see iniquity nor gird its loins for the inevitable struggle. But at last we stand with our faces to the light. At last we have faced our duty. Now it behooves us to do this duty with masterful efficiency.

We are in the war. But we are not yet awake. We are passing through, in exaggerated form, the phase through which England passed during the first year of the war. A very large number of Englishmen fooled themselves with the idea that they lived on an island and were safe anyhow; that the war would soon be over, and that if they went on with their business as usual and waved flags and applauded patriotic speeches somebody else would do the fighting for them. England has seen the error of her way; she has paid in blood and agony for her shortsightedness; she is now doing her duty with stern resolution. We are repeating her early errors on a larger scale; and assuredly we shall pay heavily if we do not in time awake from our short-sighted apathy and foolish, self-sufficient optimism.

We live on a continent. We have trusted to that fact for safety in the past; we do not understand that world

[1] From the speech delivered before the Moose Convention at Pittsburgh, July 26, 1917.

THEODORE ROOSEVELT

conditions have changed, and that the oceans and even the air have become highways for military aggression. The exploits of the German U-boat off Nantucket last summer —exploits which nothing but feebleness, considerations of political expediency, and downright lack of courage on our part permitted—showed that if Germany or any other possible opponent of ours were free to deal with us, the security that an ocean barrier once offered was annihilated. In other words, the battle front of Europe is slowly spreading over the whole world. Unless we beat Germany in Europe, we shall have to fight her deadly ambition on our own coasts and in our own continent. A great American army in Europe now is the best possible insurance against a great European or Asiatic army in our own country a couple of years or a couple of decades hence.

THE RIDERLESS HORSE
HAROLD T. PULSIFER

Close ranks and ride on!
Though his saddle be bare,
The bullet is sped,
Now the dead
Cannot care.
Close ranks and ride on!
Let the pitiless stride
Of the host that he led,
Though his saddle be red,
Sweep on like the tide.
Close ranks and ride on!
The banner he bore
For God and the right

Never faltered before.
Quick, up with it, then!
For the right! For the light!
Lest legions of men
Be lost in the night!

A CAVALRY CATCH
WILLIAM SHARP

Up! for the bugles are calling,
  Saddle, to boot, and away!
Sabres are clanking, and lances are glancing,
The colonel is swearing and horses are prancing
  So up with the sabres and lances,
    Up and away!

Where are we off to, say?
  Saddle, and boot, and away!
With a thunder of hoofs in a rush we go past,
In a whirlwind of dust we are gone as a blast —
  For we're off with the sabres and lances,
    Off and away!

A LULLABY
G. R. GLASGOW

Because some men in khaki coats
  Are marching out to war,
Beneath a torn old flag that floats
  As proudly as before;
Because they will not stop or stay,
  But march with eager tread,
A little baby far away
  Sleeps safely in her bed.

A LULLABY

Because some grim, gray sentinels
   Stand always silently,
Where each dull shadow falls and swells,
   Upon a restless sea;
Because their lonely watch they keep,
   With keen and wakeful eyes,
A little child may safely sleep
   Until the sun shall rise.

Because some swift and shadowy things
   Hold patient guard on high,
Like birds or sails or shielding wings
   Against a stormy sky;
Because a strange light spreads and sweeps
   Across a darkened way,
A little baby softly sleeps
   Until the dawn of day.

OUR COMMON HERITAGE[1]

ARTHUR J. BALFOUR

Will you permit me, on behalf of my friends and myself, to offer you my deepest and sincerest thanks for the rare and valued honor which you have done us by receiving us here to-day? We all feel the greatness of this honor, but I think to none of us can it come home so closely as to one who, like myself, has been for forty-three years in the service of a free assembly like your own. I rejoice to think that a member—a very old member, I am sorry to say—of the British House of Commons has been received here to-day by this great sister assembly with such kindness as you have shown to me and to my friends.

Ladies and gentlemen, these two assemblies are the greatest and the oldest in the world of the free assemblies now governing great nations. The history indeed of the two is very different. The beginnings of the British House of Commons go back to a dim historic past, and its full rights and status have only been conquered and permanently secured after centuries of political struggle. Your fate has been a happier one. You were called into existence at a much later stage of social development. You came into being complete and perfected and all your powers determined, and your place in the Constitution secured beyond chance of revolution; but, though the history of these two great assemblies is different, each of them represents the great democratic principle to which

[1] Delivered before the House of Representatives, Washington, on May 5, 1917.

ARTHUR JAMES BALFOUR

we look forward as the security for the future peace of the world. All of the free assemblies now to be found governing the great nations of the earth have been modeled either upon your practice or upon ours, or upon both combined.

Mr. Speaker, the compliment paid to the mission from Great Britain by such an assembly and upon such an occasion is one not one of us is ever likely to forget, but there is something, after all, even deeper and more significant in the circumstances under which I now have the honor to address you, than any which arise out of the interchange of courtesies, however sincere, between two great and friendly nations. We all, I think, feel instinctively that this is one of the great moments in the history of the world and that what is now happening on both sides of the Atlantic represents the drawing together of great and free peoples for mutual protection against the aggression of military despotism.

I am not one of those and none of you are among those who are such bad democrats as to say that democracies make no mistakes. All free assemblies have made blunders; sometimes they have committed crimes. Why is it, then, that we look forward to the spread of free institutions throughout the world, and especially among our present enemies, as one of the greatest guaranties of the future peace of the world?

I will say to you, gentlemen, how it seems to me.

It is quite true that the people and the representatives of the people may be betrayed by some momentary gust of passion into a policy which they ultimately deplore, but it is only a military despotism of the German type that can, through generations, if need be, pursue steadily, remorselessly, unscrupulously, and appallingly the object of dominating the civilization of mankind.

And, mark you, this evil, this menace under which we are now suffering, is not one which diminishes with the growth of knowledge and progress of material civilization, but on the contrary it increases with them.

When I was young, we used to flatter ourselves that progress inevitably meant peace, and that growth of knowledge was always accompanied as its natural fruit by the growth of good will among the nations of the earth. Unhappily we know better now, and we know there is such a thing in the world as a power which can, with unvarying persistence, focus all the resources of knowledge and of civilization into the one great task of making itself the moral and material master of the world.

It is against that danger that we, the free peoples of western civilization, have banded ourselves together.

It is in that great cause that we are going to fight and are fighting at this very moment side by side. In that cause we shall surely conquer; and our children will look back to this fateful date as the one from which democracies can feel secure that their progress, their civilization, their rivalry, if need be, will be conducted, not on German lines, but in the friendly and Christian spirit which really befits the age in which we live.

Mr. Speaker, ladies and gentlemen, I beg most sincerely to repeat again how heartily I thank you for the cordial welcome which you have given us to-day, and to repeat my profound sense of the significance of this unique meeting.

PEACE HYMN FOR ENGLAND AND AMERICA
GEORGE HUNTINGTON

Two empires by the sea,
Two nations great and free,
    One anthem raise.
One race of ancient fame,
One tongue, one faith, we claim;
One God, whose glorious name
    We love and praise.

What deeds our fathers wrought,
What battles we have fought,
    Let fame record.
Now, vengeful passion cease,
Come, victories of peace;
Nor hate nor pride's caprice
    Unsheathe the sword.

Though deep the sea, and wide,
'Twixt realm and realm, its tide
    Binds strand and strand.
So be the gulf between
Gray coasts and islands green
With bonds of peace serene
    And friendship spanned.

Now, may the God above
Guard the dear land we love,
    Both east and west.
Let love more fervent glow
As peaceful ages go,
And strength yet stronger grow,
    Blessing and blest.

MALBROUK—ET NOUS

When the great Duke Marlborough took the field
The ladies waved and the belfries pealed,
The cottars shouted from roofs and ricks,
The drum-boys flourished their polished sticks,
The cymbals clashed and the trumpets played
A brazen, clarion fanfarade.
Behind the lumbering cannon paced
The scarlet infantry, frogged and laced;
In velvets, ruffles and crimped perukes
The noble gentlemen of the Duke's
Terrible cavalry jingled by,
With banners splendid against the sky.

War is not what it was of yore;
Our trumpets lie in the Depôt store,
Our colors hang in the Depôt mess,
We're not conspicuous in our dress.
Leather and khaki, drab and tan
Is the *dernier cri* for a fighting man;
But we like our noise, and we make a band
Of any old thing that comes to hand,
And we throw our chests and we shift our shins
To penny-whistles and biscuit tins.
Though we drum to war on a biscuit lid
We'll do as the great Duke Marlborough did.

—From *Punch*

THE MEMORIAL DAY ADDRESS[1]
WOODROW WILSON

The program has conferred an unmerited dignity upon the remarks I am going to make by calling them an address, because I am not here to deliver an address. I am here merely to show in my official capacity the sympathy of this great Government with the object of this occasion, and also to speak just a word of the sentiment that is in my own heart.

Any memorial day of this sort is, of course, a day touched with sorrowful memory, and yet I for one do not see how we can have any thought of pity for the men whose memory we honor to-day. I do not pity them. I envy them, rather, because their great work for liberty is accomplished, and we are in the midst of a work unfinished, testing our strength where their strength already has been tested.

There is a touch of sorrow, but there is also a touch of reassurance in a day like this, because we know how the men of America have responded to the call of the cause of liberty, and it fills our mind with a perfect assurance that that response will come again in equal measures, with equal majesty, and with a result which will hold the attention of all mankind.

When you reflect upon it, these men who died to preserve the Union died to preserve the instrument which we are now using to serve the world—a free nation espousing the cause of human liberty. In one sense the great

[1] From the speech delivered May 30, 1917.

struggle into which we have now entered is an American struggle, because it is in defense of American honor and American rights, but it is something even greater than that; it is a world struggle. It is the struggle of men who love liberty everywhere; and in this cause America will show herself greater than ever because she will rise to a greater thing.

We have said in the beginning that we planned this great Government that men who wish freedom might have a place of refuge and a place where their hope could be realized, and now, having established such a Government, having preserved such a Government, having vindicated the power of such a Government, we are saying to all mankind, "We did not set this Government up in order that we might have a selfish and separate liberty, for we are now ready to come to your assistance and fight out upon the fields of the world the cause of human liberty."

No man can be glad that such things have happened as we have witnessed in these last fateful years, but perhaps it may be permitted to us to be glad that we have an opportunity to show the principles which we profess to be living—principles which live in our hearts—and to have a chance by pouring out of our blood and treasure to vindicate the things which we have professed. For, my friends, the real fruition of life is to do the things we have said we wished to do. There are times when words seem empty and only action seems great. Such a time has come, and in the providence of God, America will once more have an opportunity to show to the world that she was born to serve mankind.

GETTYSBURG ADDRESS
ABRAHAM LINCOLN

Fourscore and seven years ago our fathers brought forth on this continent a new nation, conceived in liberty and dedicated to the proposition that all men are created equal.

Now we are engaged in a great civil war, testing whether that nation, or any nation so conceived and so dedicated, can long endure. We are met on a great battle field of that war. We have come to dedicate a portion of that field as a final resting place for those who here gave their lives that that nation might live. It is altogether fitting and proper that we should do this.

But, in a larger sense, we can not dedicate—we can not consecrate—we can not hallow—this ground. The brave men, living and dead, who struggled here, have consecrated it far above our poor power to add or detract. The world will little note nor long remember what we say here, but it can never forget what they did here. It is for us, the living, rather, to be dedicated here to the unfinished work which they who fought here have thus far so nobly advanced. It is rather for us to be here dedicated to the great task remaining before us—that from these honored dead we take increased devotion to that cause for which they gave the last full measure of devotion—that we here highly resolve that these dead shall not have died in vain—that this nation, under God, shall have a new birth of freedom—and that government of the people, by the people, for the people, shall not perish from the earth.

ABRAHAM LINCOLN WALKS AT MIDNIGHT
(In Springfield, Illinois)
VACHEL LINDSAY

It is portentous, and a thing of state
That here at midnight, in our little town
A mourning figure walks, and will not rest,
Near the old courthouse pacing up and down,

Or by his homestead, or in shadowed yards
He lingers where his children used to play,
Or through the market, on the well-worn stones
He stalks until the dawn-stars burn away.

A bronzed, lank man! His suit of ancient black,
A famous high top-hat and plain worn shawl
Make him the quaint great figure that men love,
The prairie-lawyer, master of us all.

He cannot sleep upon his hillside now.
He is among us:—as in times before!
And we who toss and lie awake for long
Breathe deep, and start, to see him pass the door.

His head is bowed. He thinks on men and kings.
Yea, when the sick world cries, how can he sleep?
Too many peasants fight, they know not why,
Too many homesteads in black terror weep.

The sins of all the war-lords burn his heart.
He sees the dreadnaughts scouring every main.
He carries on his shawl-wrapped shoulders now
The bitterness, the folly and the pain.

He cannot rest until a spirit-dawn
Shall come;—the shining hope of Europe free:
The league of sober folk, the Workers' Earth,
Bringing long peace to Cornland, Alp and Sea.

It breaks his heart that kings must murder still,
That all his hours of travail here for men
Seem yet in vain. And who will bring white peace
That he may sleep upon his hill again?

UNION
VIRGINIA FRASER BOYLE

Out of the mists and the storms of the years,
Out of the glory of triumph and tears,
Out of the ashes of hope and of fears,
    The Old South still leads on.

She is bringing to-day what her hands have wrought,
What her mother's heart at her knee has taught —
Her treasure of time that her blood has bought —
    To lay at the Nation's feet.

Not the tattered things which she waves to-day —
Not the Stars and Bars she has laid away,
Nor the bended forms in their coats of gray —
    Her wondrous pledge to the past;

But the spirit that stirs through the dust of the grave,
Wherever the flags of the Union wave;
The valor the God of her heroes gave
    To freedom and liberty.

She comes with the cry that led her on,
When freedom and liberty first were born —
And the name of her peerless Washington —
  The rugged strength of her days.

She has kept unmixed, through her years of pain
America's blood in its purest vein;
As she gave to the past, she gives again
  For the glory of her land.

With a patriot's faith in the days to be,
She is pressing the seal of destiny
With the fame of her Jackson and her Lee —
  The heritage of her sons.

And she sees in her ruddy boy to-day,
In his khaki coat, her lad in gray,
And back of the drums her heartstrings play,
  When the bugles shout and call.

But her mother love is not dismayed —
She has laid her treasure unafraid
On the shrine where the sad-eyed Lincoln prayed
  That the Union might not break.

How they troop, that host that can never die!
A nation's heroes passing by —
The spirits that brook nor earth nor sky —
  For the deathless dead have heard:

They are marching out with a shadowy lance,
With the sons of sons to the fields of France;

UNION 65

And they stand at the guns while the bullets glance,
    Where England fights to win.

Oh! hallowed earth of the brave and the free —
Oh! pledges of life and liberty —
They are keeping the tryst on the land and the sea,
    Of a nation forever one!

Read in Washington to Veterans of the Confederacy, 1917.

SUPPORTING THE GOVERNMENT[1]
ELIHU ROOT

The declaration of war between the United States and Germany completely changed the relations of all the inhabitants of this country to the subject of peace and war.

Before the declaration everybody had a right to discuss in private and in public the question whether the United States should carry on war against Germany. Everybody had a right to argue that there was no sufficient cause for war, that the consequences of war would be worse than the consequences of continued peace, that it would be wiser to submit to the aggressions of Germany against American rights, that it would be better to have Germany succeed than to have the allies succeed in the great conflict.

Everybody holding these views had a right by expressing them to seek to influence public opinion and to affect the action of the President and the Congress, to whom the people of the country by their constitution have entrusted the power to determine whether the United States shall or shall not make war.

But the question of peace or war has now been decided by the President and Congress, the sole authorities which had the right to decide, the lawful authorities who rested under the duty to decide. The question no longer remains open. It has been determined and the United States is at war with Germany.

The decision was made by overwhelming majorities of both houses of Congress. When such a decision has been

---
[1] From the speech delivered at Chicago September 14, 1917.

ELIHU ROOT

made the duties—and therefore the rights—of all the people of the country immediately change.

It becomes their duty to stop discussion upon the question decided, and to act, to proceed immediately to do everything in their power to enable the government of their country to succeed in the war upon which the country has entered.

It is a fundamental necessity of government that it shall have the power to decide great questions of policy and to act upon its decision. In order that there shall be action following a decision once made, the decision must be accepted. Discussion upon the question must be deemed closed.

A nation which declares war and goes on discussing whether it ought to have declared war or not is impotent, paralyzed, imbecile, and earns the contempt of mankind and the certainty of humiliating defeat and subjection to foreign control.

A democracy which cannot accept its own decisions, made in accordance with its own laws, but must keep on endlessly discussing questions already decided, has failed in the fundamental requirements of self-government; and, if the decision is to make war, the failure to exhibit capacity for self-government by action will inevitably result in the loss of the right of self-government.

Before the decision of a proposal to make war, men may range themselves upon one side or the other of the question; but after the decision in favor of war, is made, the country has ranged itself, and the only issue left for the individual citizen is whether he is for or against his country. From that time on arguments against the war in which the country is engaged are enemy arguments.

There are doubtless some who do not understand what this struggle really is. Some who were born here resent interference with their comfort and prosperity, and the demands for sacrifice which seem to them unnecessary and they fail to see that the time has come when, if Americans are to keep the independence and liberty which their fathers won by suffering and sacrifice, they in their turn must fight again for the preservation of that independence and liberty.

Somebody has to decide where armies are to fight, whether our territory is to be defended by waiting here until we are attacked or by going out and attacking the enemy before they get here. The power to make that decision and the duty to make it rest under the constitution of this country with the President as commander-in-chief.

When the President has decided that the best way to beat Germany is to send American troops to France and Belgium, that is the way the war must be carried on, if at all. I think the decision was wise. Others may think it unwise. But, when the decision has been made, what we think is immaterial. The commander-in-chief, with all the advice and all the wisdom he can command, has decided when and where the American army is to move. The army must obey, and all loyal citizens of the country will do their utmost to make that movement a success.

This is a war of defense. It is perfectly described in the words of the constitution which established this nation: "To provide for the common defense" and "To secure the blessings of liberty to ourselves and our posterity."

The national defense demands not merely force, but

SUPPORTING THE GOVERNMENT 69

intelligence. It requires foresight, consideration of the policies and purposes of other nations, understanding of the inevitable or probable consequences of the acts of other nations, judgment as to the time when successful defense may be made, and when it will be too late, and prompt action before it is too late.

For many years we have pursued our peaceful course of internal development protected in a variety of ways. We were protected by the law of nations to which all civilized governments have professed their allegiance. So long as we committed no injustice ourselves we could not be attacked without a violation of that law.

We were protected by a series of treaties under which all the principal nations of the earth agreed to respect our rights and to maintain friendship with us. We were protected by an extensive system of arbitration created by or consequent upon the peace conferences at The Hague, and under which all controversies arising under the law and under treaties were to be settled peaceably by arbitration and not by force.

We were protected by the broad expanse of ocean separating us from all great military powers, and by the bold assertion of the Monroe Doctrine that if any of those powers undertook to overpass the ocean and establish itself upon these western continents that would be regarded as dangerous to the peace and safety of the United States, and would call upon her to act in her defense.

We were protected by the fact that the policy and the fleet of Great Britain were well known to support the Monroe Doctrine. We were protected by the delicate balance of power in Europe which made it seem not worth while for any power to engage in a conflict here at the risk of suffering from its rivals there. All these protections were swept away by the war which began in Europe in 1914.

America's independence would be gone unless she was ready to fight for it, and her security would thenceforth be not a security of freedom, but only a security purchased by submission.

Congress has been in continuous session passing with unprecedented rapidity laws containing grants of power and of money unexampled in our history. The executive establishment has been straining every nerve to prepare for war. The ablest and strongest leaders of industrial activity have been called from all parts of the country to aid the government.

The people of the country have generously responded with noble loyalty and enthusiasm to the call for the surrender of money and of customary rights, and the supply of men to the service of the country.

This is no ordinary war which the world is waging. It is no contest for petty policies and profits. It is a mighty and all-embracing struggle between two conflicting principles of human right and human duty.

It is a conflict between the divine right of kings to govern mankind through armies and nobles and the right of the peoples of the earth to toil and endure and aspire to govern themselves by law in the freedom of individual manhood.

It is the climax of the supreme struggle between autocracy and democracy. No nation can stand aside and be free from its effects. The two systems cannot endure together in the same world.

SUPPORTING THE GOVERNMENT

If autocracy triumphs, military power lustful of dominion, supreme in strength, intolerant of human rights, holding itself superior to law, to morals, to faith, to compassion, will crush out the free democracies of the world. If autocracy is defeated and nations are compelled to recognize the rules of law and of morals, then and then only will democracy be safe.

To this great conflict for human rights and human liberty America has committed herself. There can be no backward step. There must be either humiliating and degrading submission or terrible defeat or glorious victory. It was no human will that brought us to this pass. It was not the President. It was not Congress. It was not the press. It was not any political party. It was not any section or part of our people.

It was that in the providence of God the mighty forces that determine the destinies of mankind beyond the control of human purpose have brought to us the time, the occasion, the necessity, that this peaceful people so long enjoying the blessings of liberty and justice for which their fathers fought and sacrificed shall again gird themselves for conflict, and with all the forces of manhood nurtured and strengthened by liberty offer again the sacrifice of possessions and of life itself, that this nation may still be free, that the mission of American democracy shall not have failed, that the world shall be free.

> Breathes there the man, with soul so dead,
> Who never to himself hath said,
>   This is my own, my native land?
> Whose heart hath ne'er within him burned,

As home his footsteps he hath turned
    From wandering on a foreign strand?
If such there breathe, go, mark him well;
For him no minstrel raptures swell;
High though his titles, proud his name,
Boundless his wealth as wish can claim,—
Despite those titles, power, and pelf,
The wretch, concentred all in self,
Living, shall forfeit fair renown,
And, doubly dying, shall go down
To the vile dust from whence he sprung,
Unwept, unhonored, and unsung.

—From Scott's "Lay of the Last Minstrel"

"OF OLD SAT FREEDOM ON THE HEIGHTS
ALFRED TENNYSON

Of old sat Freedom on the heights,
    The thunders breaking at her feet:
Above her shook the starry lights:
    She heard the torrents meet.

There in her place she did rejoice,
    Self-gather'd in her prophet-mind,
But fragments of her mighty voice
    Came rolling on the wind.

Then stept she down thro' town and field
    To mingle with the human race,
And part by part to men reveal'd
    The fulness of her face —

Grave mother of majestic works,
  From her isle-altar gazing down,
Who, God-like, grasps the triple forks,
  And King-like, wears the crown:

Her open eyes desire the truth.
  The wisdom of a thousand years
Is in them. May perpetual youth
  Keep dry their light from tears;

That her fair form may stand and shine,
  Make bright our days and light our dreams,
Turning to scorn with lips divine
  The falsehood of extremes!

THE PRESENT CRISIS
JAMES RUSSELL LOWELL

Once to every man and nation comes the moment to decide,
In the strife of Truth with Falsehood, for the good or evil side;
Some great cause, God's new Messiah, offering each the bloom or blight,
Parts the goats upon the left hand, and the sheep upon the right,
And the choice goes by forever 'twixt that darkness and that light.

* * * * * * * * *

Hast thou chosen, O my people, on whose party thou shalt stand,
Ere the Doom from its worn sandals shakes the dust against our land?

Though the cause of Evil prosper, yet 'tis Truth alone is strong,
And, albeit she wander outcast now, I see around her throng
Troops of beautiful, tall angels, to enshield her from all wrong.

* * * * * * * *

Careless seems the great Avenger; history's pages but record
One death-grapple in the darkness 'twixt old systems and the Word;
Truth forever on the scaffold, Wrong forever on the throne,—
Yet that scaffold sways the future, and, behind the dim unknown,
Standeth God within the shadow, keeping watch above his own.

* * * * * * * *

CARRY ON!

ROBERT W. SERVICE

It's easy to fight when everything's right,
And you're mad with the thrill and the glory;
It's easy to cheer when victory's near,
And wallow in fields that are gory.
It's a different song when everything's wrong,
When you're feeling infernally mortal;
When it's ten against one, and hope there is none,
Buck up, little soldier, and chortle:

CARRY ON!

    Carry on! Carry on!
  There isn't much punch in your blow.
You're glaring and staring and hitting out blind;
You're muddy and bloody, but never you mind.
    Carry on! Carry on!
  You haven't the ghost of a show.
It's looking like death, but while you've a breath,
    Carry on, my son! Carry on!

And so in the strife of the battle of life
It's easy to fight when you're winning;
It's easy to slave, and starve and be brave,
When the dawn of success is beginning.
But the man who can meet despair and defeat
With a cheer, there's the man of God's choosing;
The man who can fight to Heaven's own height
Is the man who can fight when he's losing.

    Carry on! Carry on!
  Things never were looming so black.
But show that you haven't a cowardly streak,
And though you're unlucky you never are weak
    Carry on! Carry on!
  Brace up for another attack.
It's looking like hell, but—you never can tell:
    Carry on, old man! Carry on!

CHANGES AHEAD[1]
MARION LeROY BURTON

When we speak of changes that are ahead, the most serious question which you and I must meet is, Can the democratic American government be made efficient? That is the question that has been raised about democratic government from the days of Plato to the present. You and I know that it is a little difficult for us at times to assert, without any qualifications, that democracy can be made efficient. When one thinks of the scandal of American politics, of the corruption, the bribery, the intrigue, and the duplicity, then it is not possible for him to consider with great composure some of the things that are said by the keen, discriminating persons who try to find out whether we are wise, economical, and efficient in the administration of our affairs. Think of the Philadelphia Gas ring, think of the Tweed ring, think of New York city at the present moment. Think of the beautiful capitol of the great Empire state of New York, costing hundreds of thousands of dollars, with its magnificently carved mahogany ceilings — until one day a janitor accidentally slipped off a rafter and his feet went through brown paper!

You and I are perfectly aware of the fact that these are only superficial observations and comments upon politics and statesmanship and municipal administration in America. You and I must admit, candidly and frankly, that all of these things can be said with remarkable

---
[1] From the speech delivered at St.Cloud, Minn., October 17, 1917.

Marion LeRoy Burton

Marina in her Boudoir

accuracy about our government. But you and I know something that most of our foreign critics never sense. They always interpret us in the terms of our successful and superficial materialism, and they do not come to see that back of all of these external things there is here the finest spirit of idealism that permeates any nation of the world to-day.

You and I know that American government is not what the carping critic says it is, but we know that it is what you and I dream in our best moments it shall be when we have brought to pass the things for which we are striving; that is what American government really is. It is just what you and I determine it shall be.

But there is another change which we must meet, and it is the thing which gives me pause and serious concern. Somehow we must get to the one hundred millions of our people a new conception of what democracy really is. You and I have imagined in the past that democracy is a form of government which is responsible to the people. That is true. But we must see that there are two sides to this shield. We must recognize on the one hand that the government which we make is responsible to us. But more and more, particularly in times of war, we must understand too that the people are responsible to the government.

Now how are we going to get that? How are we going to have the people see that once they have constituted government, then it is their duty to be loyal to that authority and to place at its disposal absolutely everything they have? For in this time of war our duty is not simply the making of a great army, but it is recognizing clearly the principle of the selective draft, that every man, woman, and child within the confines of the United States of America must deliver his full strength for the government. It is a question of putting an entire nation of one hundred million people under arms. Somehow, some way, you and I, as those who are responsible for communities, must see to it that our people get a deepened consciousness of their individual responsibility. Now how are we going to secure such a result?

One way we are going to get it is to have them see the clearness, the seriousness, and the finality of the issue in which we are now engaged. Why, men, it is absolutely final. We are witnessing the death grapple of two of the most gigantic ideas that have ever animated conflicting nations. On the one side is ruthlessness and frightfulness and barbarism and militarism and autocracy, and on the other side is good will and brotherhood and freedom and equality and education and opportunity and democracy.

Is there any question as to where we ought to stand? Are there two sides to this issue? Sometimes a man has the stupidity to say to me that he is not pro-German but that he is against the war. Before he can get his mouth shut I say to him, "You are pro-German, for 'he that is not for us is against us.'"

If ever there was any truth in the sayings of our Master there is truth in this one, "Ye cannot serve God and mammon." If there was ever a holy war this is a holy war!

Do you suppose that we are in this war for conquest or for territory? We are not out for conquest, or for the crushing of any people, or with any false motive, but we have gone into this war for just what President Wilson said, "to make the world safe for democracy." We must recognize that upon the solution of the problems of Central Europe hangs the fate of American civilization.

HYMN OF FREEDOM
MARY PERRY KING

Unfurl the flag of Freedom,
    Fling far the bugle blast!
There comes a sound of marching
    From out the mighty past.
Let every peak and valley
    Take up the valiant cry:
Where, beautiful as morning
    Our banner cuts the sky.

Free-born to peace and justice,
    We stand to guard and save
The liberty of manhood,
    The faith our fathers gave.
Then soar aloft, Old Glory,
    And tell the waiting breeze
No law but Right and Mercy
    Shall rule the Seven Seas.

No hate is in our anger,
    No vengeance in our wrath,
We hold the line of freedom
    Across the tyrant's path.
Where'er oppression vaunteth
    We loose the sword once more
To stay the feet of conquest,
    And pray an end of war.

PATRIOTISM
LYMAN ABBOTT

A nation is made great, not by its fruitful acres, but by the men who cultivate them; not by its great forests, but by the men who use them; not by its mines, but by the men who work in them; not by its railways, but by the men who build and run them. America was a great land when Columbus discovered it; Americans have made it a great Nation.

In 1776 our fathers had a vision of a new Nation "conceived in liberty and dedicated to the proposition that all men are created equal." Without an army they fought the greatest of existing world empires that they might realize this vision. A third of a century later without a navy they fought the greatest navy in the world, that they might win for their Nation the freedom of the seas. Half a century later they fought through an unparalleled Civil War that they might establish for all time on this continent the inalienable right of life, liberty, and the pursuit of happiness. A third of a century later they fought to emancipate an oppressed neighbor, and, victory won, gave back Cuba to the Cubans, sent an army of schoolmasters to educate for liberty the Filipinos, asked no war indemnity from their vanquished enemy, but paid him liberally for his property. Meanwhile they offered land freely to any farmer who would live upon and cultivate it, opened to foreign immigrants on equal terms the door of industrial opportunity, shared with them political equality, and provided by universal taxation for universal education.

Photo by Brown Bros.

LYMAN ABBOTT

The cynic who can see in this history only a theme for his egotistical satire is no true American, whatever his parentage, whatever his birthplace. He who looks with pride upon this history which his fathers have written by their heroic deeds, who accepts with gratitude the inheritance which they have bequeathed to him, and who highly resolves to preserve this inheritance unimpaired and to pass it on to his descendants enlarged and enriched, is a true American, be his birthplace or his parentage what it may.

—From *The Outlook*, June, 1916

EARTH CALLS TO HEAVEN
WILLIAM PIERSON MERRILL

God, to Thee Thy earth is calling
  With a stern and bitter cry.
Hatred, anguish, death appalling
  In thick clouds about us lie.
All the youth are fighting, falling,
  Driven forth in bands to die.

Wilt Thou make an end forever?
  Shall the horror never cease?
Wilt Thou not to souls imprisoned
  Speak the word that brings release —
Shining through the storm of sorrow
  Set the rainbow of Thy peace?

Yet if only by such anguish
  Can Thy righteous peace be won,
Spare us not, O God of justice;

Finish what Thou hast begun.
Make us bear the loss of all things,
So Thy holy will be done.

Let not all the wounds be wasted,
Nor these dead have died in vain;
By this war let war be smitten,
Nevermore to rise again;
Set above all kings triumphant
Him Whose right it is to reign.

Let our Babel lie in fragments,
Shattered by Thine iron rod;
Let a mighty growth of freedom
Blossom from the blood-soaked sod;
On the ruin of the nations
Rear the Commonwealth of God.

—From *The Continent*

THE LITTLE STAR IN THE WINDOW
JOHN JEROME ROONEY

There's a little star in the window of the house across the way,
A little star, red-bordered, on a ground of pearly white;
I can see its gleam at evening; it is bright at dawn of day,
And I know it has been shining through the long and dismal night.

The folks who pass the window on the busy city street,
I often notice, turn a glance before they hurry by,

THE LITTLE STAR IN THE WINDOW

And one, a gray haired woman, made curtsey low and sweet,
While something like a teardrop was glistening in her eye.

And yesterday an aged man, by life's stern battle spent
His empty coat sleeve hanging down, a witness sadly mute,
Gave one swift look and halted — his form full height, unbent —
And ere he passed his hand came up in soldierly salute.

The little star in the window is aflame with living fire,
For it was lit at the hearthstone where a lonely mother waits;
And she has stained its crimson with the glow of her heart's desire,
And brightened its pearl white heaven beyond the world's dark hates.

The star shall shine through the battle when the shafts of death are hurled;
It shall shine through the long night watches in the foremost trenches' line;
Over the waste of waters and beyond the verge of the world,
Like the guiding Star of the Magi its blessed rays shall shine.

The little star in the window shall beacon your boy's return
As his eyes are set to the homeland, when the call of the guns shall cease;

In the Flag's high constellation through the ages it shall burn,
A pledge of his heart's devotion, a sign of his people's peace.

"Our Father's God! from out whose hand
The centuries fall like grains of sand,
    *   *   *   *   *
Oh, make Thou us, through centuries long,
In peace secure, in justice strong:
Around our gift of freedom draw
The safeguards of Thy righteous law:
And, cast in some diviner mold,
Let the new cycle shame the old."

—From Whittier's "Centennial Hymn"

THE BATTLE BETWEEN RIGHT AND MIGHT[1]

FRANK O. LOWDEN

If this war in which we are engaged shall go against us, every oration which has commemorated the efforts and the greatness of Washington must be revised. Instead of representing him, the noblest figure, as someone has said, who ever stood in the forefront of a nation's life, we shall have to set him down as one of those idle dreamers who dreamed of great things in vain, and whom a practical world has relegated to oblivion. There is not a thing for which he stood, there is not a hope which he ever entertained, there is not an idea of government for which he fought during those years of the Revolutionary War, that will not become obsolete if the Central Empires win in this war which is flaming all about the world.

I want to remind you to-day that we are going through no more gloomy time than Washington, year after year, plodded through. And I want also to remind you that Washington—even Washington—could he have had his way and ended the war as early as he desired, would have missed the greatest service that in the end he rendered to humanity and the world. He was not for the separation of the colonies from the mother land. He said, time and time again in the early months of the war, that the colonies had no desire to set up independence, but that all they wished was to have the legal rights which they believed they were entitled to accorded to them by His Majesty's government in London.

[1] From the speech delivered before the Union League Club of Chicago, February 22, 1918.

Washington hoped that this bitter war between daughter and mother might come to an end. And, as we look back now, we know that if Lexington and Concord and Bunker Hill had been won overwhelmingly by the Colonists, independence would not have come to the United States; there would have been a reconciliation in all likelihood, and to-day instead of the proud, independent position we occupy among the nations of the earth, we would have been but a dependent of an empire across the sea.

Oh, as we review the years of our history, no one can resist the conviction that there has been a divine guidance in all the great crises of our national life. It was necessary that we should lose Bunker Hill; it was necessary that our armies should retreat year after year in order that the colonists might be compelled to declare independence from all nations and to set up for themselves.

And when we come to the other great crisis in our life, the same was true. Lincoln had no intention, at the beginning of the Civil War, to abolish slavery. He said, time and time again, that the South was entitled under the constitution to the protection of slavery within the States where it existed. And, again, if we had won overwhelmingly the first battles of the Civil War, slavery would have remained, and the great accomplishment of Lincoln's life would not have been. It was necessary that our southern friends should fight, and fight so valiantly that, simply as a war measure, we would be compelled, in order to survive, to declare the emancipation of the slaves.

Again, those darkest years of the Civil War, years which some of you are old enough to recall, were not in vain, and we passed through the darkness and the shadow in order that the high accomplishment of the freedom of four million slaves might come.

And in this war, this war which girdles the very globe, there is some divine purpose hidden though it be, that requires us, following the example of Washington and Lincoln, to persist, no matter how dark the skies may be, until a final and decisive victory, which shall mean peace for ourselves and for our children for all time to come.

It is the final battle, not only between the forces of autocracy and the forces of democracy, but it is the final battle between the forces of evil and the forces of righteousness. It is the final conflict between justice and injustice. It is the final battle, which is to settle whether men, all men, whatever their condition in life, are entitled to their own liberty; whether they are entitled to rule themselves; or whether the great masses of mankind must toil, toil everlastingly, in order that a few thousands may enjoy the blessings of the earth.

That is what this war means, and there is no spot in all the earth so obscure that that spot can escape its consequences. It is just as fatal to America as it is to England, or France or Italy, if we lose this war.

I do not mean to say that we might not, for a few years, maintain the form of our government; but its substance and its spirit would be gone; the freedom which has been our dearest possession all these years would have flown. We would listen to what the Imperial powers of Berlin might permit us to hear; we would read, as their own people do, the doctrines which had had Imperial approval. Our liberties we might retain in form for a few brief years, but that is all.

The war is not three thousand miles away; the war is at your door and mine this very hour. And, if we would preserve as sacred spots forevermore the tomb of Washington on the Potomac, and the tomb of Lincoln at Springfield; if we are unwilling they shall become the monuments of human folly and failure; if we are unwilling that Washington and Lincoln shall be known as fond dreamers who failed to make their dreams come true, we shall present a solidarity of our people which will absolutely insure success.

As I said a little while ago, there is some divine, if hidden, purpose in this war. We may not see it now. Washington, in the bitterness of his defeat at Long Island and his retreat from there, could not see that there was a providence in that defeat which helped him to win the independence of America. Lincoln, in the bitterness of the defeat at the first battle of Bull Run, and the disasters that followed that battle, could not foresee the divine purpose in those defeats; but we now, in the light of later years, know that those defeats were necessary if slavery should be extinguished on this continent.

Thus to-day we cannot see what the purpose is in this war, but that there is some purpose we must have the faith to believe. We do know that all was not well with us before the war came. We do know that there were great problems which we had not solved. We do know that civilization was not a complete success, even in America, before this war came on. We remember that we were becoming grossly materialistic people; and I think a thousand years from now, when the history of the nineteenth century is written, that century will be characterized as the century which developed materialism more than anything else. We became enamored of the things which are seen, of the things which we can touch. We gloried in our invention, and we believed that science would fathom all the secrets of the universe, and that science was all-sufficient for human life. When the war broke out, we found that this same science of which we boasted as the greatest asset of democracy, was the greatest resource of war. It then seemed to us as though all our progress of a century was simply for the purpose of making war more terrible and more deadly than it had been in all its past. And we began to think that maybe there are other things in the universe than the things that you can see and touch and hold.

We thought, before the war, that discipline was no longer of use. Discipline had broken down in the home, in the school, in the State; and we no longer believed that our citizenship was of priceless worth. We assumed that it was simply something that conferred privileges upon us but which exacted nothing in return. And now we see, when nations are breaking down all around us, that the dearest thing in all our possession is not a material thing at all. We are getting a new idea of what country means. We are having a revival of spiritual forces. And when this war is over, we shall have a better world than we have had in the past, I believe. The old sense of brotherhood which our fathers felt had disappeared. We were dividing into classes, forgetting that the only thing in all the world that will make men brothers is character and not possession.

How fortunate it was that the two great figures in our national past were more distinguished for character than they were for learning. How fortunate that Washington and Lincoln attained their colossal size not so much by their intellectual splendor as by their superb character.

And in a democracy, if democracy is to survive, character must always take the lead and direct the life. We shall have a better world when this war is over, and we must have the faith now to know that these sacrifices of our gallant boys are not being made in vain.

We shall win if we shall only realize what the war means. God grant that our hearts and minds may be filled with the full significance of this last great battle between the material forces and the spiritual forces of the universe.

> God, who gavest men eyes
> To see a dream;
> God, who gavest men heart
> To follow the Gleam;
> God, who gavest men stars
> To find heaven by;
> God, who madest men glad
> At need to die;
> Lord, from the hills again
> We hear thy drum!
> God, who lovest free men,
> God, who lovest free men,
> God, who lovest free men,
> Lead on! We come.

—From Hermann Hagedorn's *Ode of Dedication*

"OVER THERE!"
HARVEY M. WATTS

Some day we'll join them over there and know
  The haunting secret that lights up their face,
  Giving their humblest act a touch of grace
As if all saw the vision in the glow
Of Heaven ajar, as, lo, they cry "We go
Comrades in arms of those who set the pace,
Ready to fall if they but win the race
Ere tyranny shall strike the fateful blow." —
Some day! Ah, yes, the long way over there
We too shall tread since they have gladly gone
As pioneers and paid the final toll!
So fear we not, as if in dull despair,
To face with them the bright unending dawn,
Lest saving life we lose all else, the soul!

TO THE AMERICAN PEOPLE
BAYARD TAYLOR

That late, in half-despair, I said:
"The Nation's ancient life is dead;
Her arm is weak, her blood is cold;
She hugs the peace that gives her gold,—
The shameful peace, that sees expire
Each beacon-light of patriot fire,
And makes her court a traitors' den,"—
Forgive me this, my countrymen!

O, in your long forbearance grand,
Slow to suspect the treason planned,
Enduring wrong, yet hoping good

For sake of olden brotherhood,
How grander, how sublimer far
At the roused Eagle's call ye are,
Leaping from slumber to the fight,
For Freedom and for Chartered Right!

Throughout the land there goes a cry;
A sudden splendor fills the sky:
From every hill the banners burst,
Like buds by April breezes nurst;
In every hamlet, home, and mart,
The fire-beat of a single heart
Keeps time to strains whose pulses mix
Our blood with that of Seventy-Six!

* * * * * *

Draw forth your million blades as one;
Complete the battle then begun!
God fights with ye, and overhead
Floats the dear banner of your dead.
They, and the glories of the Past,
The Future, dawning dim and vast,
And all the holiest hopes of Man,
Are beaming triumph in your van!

Slow to resolve, be swift to do!
Teach ye the False how fight the True!
How bucklered Perfidy shall feel
In her black heart the Patriot's steel;
How sure the bolt that Justice wings;
How weak the arm a traitor brings;
How mighty they, who steadfast stand
For Freedom's Flag and Freedom's Land

THE EDUCATION WE ARE FIGHTING FOR[1]
HENRY VAN DYKE

We Americans are in this war because the claim that Germany has been chosen and empowered of God to rule the world by might does not suit us. We do not believe it. We are in this war because that claim in its contemptuous "will to power" has trampled upon our sovereign rights, has murdered our citizens upon the high seas, and has put our existence as a free republic into peril.

Do you believe that? I do not see how you can believe anything else. This world is not big enough for the existence of a system of absolute military autocracy which claims the right to rule the world by might, and the existence of a real democracy which says that there must be a government of the people, by the people, for the people.

We have been forced to fight. But do not misunderstand me; we are not fighting against the German theory of education — you can not fight against a theory, a thing of air. We are fighting against its results, treachery, violations, invasion, barbarism, cruelty, worldwide bloodshed and horror. We must show, or help to show, beside Great Britain and France, that those results are a failure and a sham. We must help to show that the world positively can not be conquered and dominated in that way. We must go with France and Great Britain, Italy and Belgium to defeat the German arms on the land and the German submarines in the sea; and when victory is won, we can profitably and honorably begin a conversation

[1] From the address before The Convocation of New York in 1918.

on peace, but not before. When that peace arrives—God grant it may be soon!—when that peace arrives, with restitution, reparation and guarantees of security for all the peoples who have suffered from the madness of the Potsdam pride, then perhaps the German people will realize that their education has been wrong and will set to work to change it.

But I must confess that I care less about the democratization of Germany, and the reform of German education, than I do about the thing which must precede them — a real victory over the kaiser's tools.

Meantime, we Americans cling to the idea of education, which has made and sustained us. Learning without conscience is a vain and noxious thing. Its only result is to create a spectacled barbarism. Man does not exist to serve the state. The state exists to protect the rights of man. All governments derive their just powers from the consent of the governed. Might does not make right, but right must gain might to survive.

To-day we are fighting for that ideal beside our brave allies. It is the ideal of our hearts; it is the ideal that is in our education; it is the ideal that every one of your public school teachers to-day is trying to give to the children; it is the ideal that every one of our universities has put into its young men, and its bachelors of arts and its maids of arts, and its mistresses of arts, and its doctors of philosophy — it has put it into them — and that is why, when this battle burst upon the world, even before we were in it, hundreds and thousands of our young American high school and college and university trained youth, boys and girls, volunteers, rushed to the flag of France to fight by her side and help her to win the victory.

And now that we are in it, who are the best men in our officers' reserve corps and in our training camps? They are the men who have come from our higher institutions of learning, where they were taught not to worship autocracy, not to believe that might is right, but to worship democracy under the guidance of a God whose right is the seal and sign of his omnipotent might.

Let us hold fast to this faith, to this ideal! Let The University of the State of New York see to it that nothing that is not democratic, free, liberal, ever comes into our education; that even in this stress of war, where we have to train soldiers to fight for peace, we do not become militaristic, we remain a democratic nation, a nation in which the state exists for the people.

To-morrow, when we have made that ideal victorious against the German foe, we shall make it safe for all the world by a league of free nations to protect peace.

A HYMN
ROBERT GRANT

O spirit of creation
    To whom our fathers prayed,
Look down upon this nation
    Whose sons go unafraid
Across the mine-strewn water
    To grapple with a foe
That makes relentless slaughter
    And agonizes woe.

Protect them, Oh, protect them,
    Our darlings blithe and brave,

But should some fate elect them
    To fill a soldier's grave,
Give us the grace to borrow
    The gladness they express
To dignify our sorrow,
    Redeem our loneliness.

We thank Thee for the vision
    Enabling us to see
That peace which brought derision
    Was ruin to the free.
At last our bonds are broken,
    At last the drum beats roll;
Ay! by this myriad token
    Our country finds her soul.

For now the heathen rages,
    And vaunting in his pride
Would blot Thee from his pages
    To rule by fratricide.
Oh, give them might to slay him
    Oh, give us faith to win,
And utterly repay him
    With knowledge of his sin.

Our flag will wear new glory
    Before our boys return,
Its crimson stripes be gory,
    Its stars like planets burn;
And many will be sleeping
    Upon a foreign shore,
Yet still within Thy keeping,
    Jehovah, God of War!

THE RETURN
JOHN FREEMAN

I heard the rumbling guns.   I saw the smoke,
  The unintelligible shock of hosts that still,
Far off, unseeing, strove and strove again;
  And beauty flying naked down the hill.

From morn to eve: and the stern night cried Peace!
  And shut the strife in darkness: all was still,
Then slowly crept a triumph on the dark —
  And I heard Beauty singing up the hill.

—From *The Westminster Gazette*

FIGHTING BATTLES WITH SPEECH AND PEN[1]
CHARLES EVANS HUGHES

It is difficult to draw nice distinctions in time of war. But there are some distinctions which must be drawn. The effective prosecution of war involves of necessity certain restrictions in our accustomed freedom. With respect to property and business, with respect to life itself, freedom is restrained. Witness our War Defense and Conscription Acts, our broad plans of regulation by which manifold activities are controlled to an unusual degree. Of course, freedom of speech and of the press is also a relative freedom. There is no license to destroy the Nation or to turn it over helpless to its foes. There is no constitutional privilege for disloyalty, or for efforts to obstruct the enforcement of the law or to interfere with the war plans adopted by authority. But with due recognition of the difficulty of exact definition and close distinction, it is quite obvious that there is a field for honest criticism which cannot be surrendered without imperiling the essentials of liberty and the preservation of the Nation itself. Our officers of Government are not a privileged class. Even when equipped with the extraordinary powers of war, they are the servants of the Nation accountable for the exercise of their authority.

When we are in the throes of war, united in the determination to win, and conscious that we can win only by united effort, there is no place for partisanship with respect

---
[1] From the speech delivered at the dinner of the American Newspaper Publishers Association in New York, April 25, 1918.

to the conduct of the war. In the phrase of Lincoln, we must meet "upon a level one step higher than any party platform" because from such more elevated position we can "do better battle for the country we love than we possibly can from those lower ones where from the force of habit, the prejudices of the past and selfish hopes of the future, we are sure to expend much of our ingenuity and strength in finding fault with and aiming blows at each other." I stand on that platform supporting the President of the United States. But that is a counsel not for Republicans alone but for Democrats as well — for those in office as well as for those out of office. We may reserve our partisan differences for other matters than the war —for policies aside from the conduct of the war. In this great crisis we bend our common strength to fight our common battle and we speak not as Democrats or as Republicans, but as citizens whose only rivalry is in their zeal to win.

Of course, it is just as easy to be a partisan in assailing criticism as in criticism itself. The man who defends everything that is done by his party or his party leaders is just as partisan as the man who assails everything that the opposing party does or plans. War demands fighting men who see straight and shoot straight. It also demands fighting critics who see straight and are honest and candid in criticism. It is a commonplace that a public officer learns more from his critics than he does from his admirers. He seldom learns from anyone but his critics. If we had to choose between partisanship with criticism and the absence of both partisanship and criticism, I should unhesitatingly choose the former, for while the venomous shafts of partisan malice seldom hit the mark, the country cannot afford to turn its destiny over to anyone who is guaranteed immunity from candid criticism.

It goes without saying that the country should have the facts. Plainly, there are matters which for military reasons must be concealed so as not to aid the enemy. But any one who conceals facts even in war time has a heavy burden of proof as to the necessity for such concealment.

Furnishing material for criticism is by no means the same thing as giving aid and comfort to the enemy. Let the truth be known. The anxiety should be not to avoid disclosure but rather to prevent error. Rarely will the enemy be the gainer from our knowledge of the facts. He will thrive on our apprehensions and our misconceptions.

The world will never be made safe for democracy, in the last analysis, by anything short of a dominant sense of fairness and justice. A contemptible purveyor of slander, of malicious abuse of officers, of half-truths calculated to deceive, of demagogical appeal in order to win affluence, influence and political power by preying upon ignorance and natural aspirations — that is the lurking enemy of our institutions which it is harder to defeat than even a Prussian autocrat. The extent of the impotency of this lurking enemy is the measure of our ultimate victory.

This is a time of rare privilege for the men who can go abroad to fight. It is also a time of rare privilege for those who stay at home to fight battles of speech and pen. Our trust is in both pen and sword—the pen to support the sword—the sword to make way for new victories of the pen. In the present situation, with Germany using up its man-power with the mad recklessness of desperation, we have a peculiar responsibility. Our Allies are holding the Western line with grim determination. They have held this line — our line — Liberty's line, the line of a world of freedom, of law, of decency, the line of all that is left of civilization as opposed to cynical force, to unparalleled brutality, to fiendish perversion of science, to the disregard of everything sacred and humane — our Allies are holding this line awaiting our arrival. They have been holding a bloody vigil. They have more dead in France than we shall have there living in arms for many months to come. But we are coming. Our forces are growing daily. We are not living in retrospect. Our faces are toward France and the future. If there was ever any doubt as to duty or opportunity there is certainly none now. Germany's only hope is that we shall falter, but we will not falter.

Let there be no thought that a great army will not be needed. The way to strike terror to the German heart, to make it realize the inevitableness of defeat, is for the United States to rush its preparations on a scale adequate to victory. Let us have a comprehensive industrial plan to insure needed direction of industrial effort, for we cannot otherwise provide the fighting men.

It is not the measure of our high calling to gather a force merely to hold a line of trenches. A peace with the German Army on the soil of France, with Germany temporarily exhausted but not beaten, cannot be lasting. A peace with Germany, leaving the German Empire through ill-gotten gains stronger relatively than when it entered the war, with a national consciousness that its policy of brutality, of disregard of treaties, of vast military preparation, has won a larger international opportunity, would be nothing but a German peace, whatever concessions might be made in the West. It is for America, by supplying an adequate number of fighting men, to make the victory decisive; to see that there is no faltering until this great duty to humanity is fully performed and the banner of a new international order, secure in the common sense of justice, waves over a world untroubled by insane dreams of arbitrary power.

GIVE US MEN!
THE BISHOP OF EXETER

Give us men!
Men from every rank,
Fresh and free and frank;
Men of thought and reading,
Men of light and leading,
Men of loyal breeding,
The Nation's welfare speeding;
Men of faith and not of faction
Men of lofty aim and action:
Give us men—I say again,
Give us men!

Give us men!
Strong and stalwart ones;
Men whom highest hope inspires,
Men whom purest honor fires,
Men who trample self beneath them,
Men who make their country wreathe them
As her noble sons.

Worthy of their sires;
Men who never shame their mothers,
Men who never fail their brothers,
True, however false are others;
Give us men—I say again,
  Give us men!

BE STRONG
MALTBIE DAVENPORT BABCOCK

Be strong!
We are not here to play, to dream, to drift.
We have hard work to do, and loads to lift.
Shun not the struggle; face it. 'T is God's gift.

Be strong!
Say not the days are evil,—who's to blame?—
And fold the hands and acquiesce—O shame!
Stand up, speak out, and bravely, in God's name.

Be strong!
It matters not how deep entrenched the wrong,
How hard the battle goes, the days how long.
Faint not, fight on! To-morrow brings the song.

THE MEN AT THE FRONT
DAVID LLOYD GEORGE

It is incredible the devotion, the valor, and the endurance of these gallant men at the front. They have given courage a new meaning; they have given it a new standard, a new rating. It means something different, something more than it ever meant before. We knew that amongst us we had a man here and a man there who had a heart of gold, and was capable of daring and enterprise, who had valor firing his soul; but that we had thousands, nay myriads of them, spread all over the land, in the highest and in the humblest homes—that is the revelation of this war—a treasure, an inexhaustible treasure, hidden in the heart of the humblest man, of patriotism, consecration, courage, devotion, exalted attachment to ideals, and readiness of sacrifice for a great purpose. We had thought these qualities were qualities of the select, but they are all great, they are all select. It is a nation of heroes. If we can do such things in war we can also do them in peace. Peace has its sacrifices; peace demands valor; peace demands devotion; and it will be an unutterable insanity if the lesson which this war has taught us of the possibilities of our people in unity, in sacrifice for a common end, in devotion to the cause of a common humanity and of our common country, should be lost when the flag has been brought back triumphant from the field of battle and planted on the field of labor and of toil.

THE CONNAUGHT RANGERS

WINIFRED M. LETTS

I saw the Connaught Rangers when they were passing by,
On a spring day, a good day, with gold rifts in the sky.
Themselves were marching steadily along the Liffey quay
An' I see the young proud look of them as if it was to-day!
The bright lads, the right lads, I have them in my mind,
With the green flags on their bayonets all fluttering in the wind!

A last look at old Ireland, a last good-bye maybe,
Then the gray sea, the wide sea, my grief upon the sea!
And when will they come home, says I, when will they see once more
The dear blue hills of Wicklow and Wexford's dim gray shore?
The brave lads of Ireland, no better lads you'll find
With the green flags on their bayonets all fluttering in the wind!

Three years have passed since that spring day, sad years for them and me.
Green graves there are in Serbia and in Gallipoli,
And many who went by that day along the muddy street
Will never hear the roadway ring to their triumphant feet.
But when they march before him, God's welcome will be kind,
And the green flags on their bayonets will flutter in the wind.

"BADDEST BOY"

People said; yes, people said
   That the baddest boy in town
Was a kid, a freckled kid,
   By the name of Willie Brown.
He disappeared; people sneered,
   And guessed it, with a frown—
"Gone to enlist—he won't be missed-
   Why, he's the baddest boy in town

         Baddest boy!
I saw him marching—
Marching
         Down the avenue!
With a step so free and easy,
And his eyes so bright and blue!
         Baddest boy!
Some one was watching—
Watching
         Willie Brown!
And I knew that she was praying for
   The baddest boy in town!

People say the other day
   Came a message to our town.
They read it out—it was about
   Private William Brown.
The message said that he was dead—
   In action he went down.
And people say he saved the day—
   The baddest boy in town!

"BADDEST BOY"

      Baddest boy!
I saw him marching—
Marching
      Down the avenue!
Behind the colors of his regiment
And the old red, white and blue!
      Baddest boy!
Some one was watching—
Watching
      Willie Brown!
And I know that she'll be mourning for
      The baddest boy in town!

FLAG-DAY ADDRESS[1]
WOODROW WILSON

My Fellow-citizens:

We meet to celebrate Flag Day because this flag which we honor and under which we serve is the emblem of our unity, our power, our thought and purpose as a nation. It has no other character than that which we give it from generation to generation. The choices are ours. It floats in majestic silence above the hosts that execute those choices, whether in peace or in war. And yet, though silent, it speaks to us—speaks to us of the past, of the men and women who went before us and of the records they wrote upon it. We celebrate the day of its birth; and from its birth until now it has witnessed a great history, has floated on high the symbol of great events, of a great plan of life worked out by a great people. We are about to carry it into battle, to lift it where it will draw the fire of our enemies. We are about to bid thousands, hundreds of thousands, it may be millions, of our men— the young, the strong, the capable men of the nation— to go forth and die beneath it on fields of blood far away— for what? For some unaccustomed thing? For something for which it has never sought the fire before? American armies were never before sent across the seas. Why are they sent now? For some new purpose for which this great flag has never been carried before, or for some old, familiar, heroic purpose for which it has seen men, its own men, die on every battlefield upon which Americans have borne arms since the Revolution?

[1] From a speech delivered June 14, 1917.

FLAG-DAY ADDRESS

These are questions which must be answered. We are Americans. We in our turn serve America, and can serve her with no private purpose. We must use her flag as she has always used it. We are accountable at the bar of history and must plead in utter frankness what purpose it is we seek to serve.

It is plain enough how we were forced into the war. The extraordinary insults and aggressions of the Imperial German Government left us no self-respecting choice but to take up arms in defense of our rights as a free people and of our honor as a sovereign Government. The military masters of Germany denied us the right to be neutral. They filled our unsuspecting communities with vicious spies and conspirators and sought to corrupt the opinion of our people in their own behalf. When they found that they could not do that, their agents diligently spread sedition amongst us and sought to draw our own citizens from their allegiance; and some of those agents were men connected with the official embassy of the German Government itself here in our own capital.

They sought by violence to destroy our industries and arrest our commerce. They tried to incite Mexico to take up arms against us and to draw Japan into a hostile alliance with her; and that, not by indirection, but by direct suggestion from the foreign office in Berlin. They impudently denied us the use of the high seas and repeatedly executed their threat that they would send to their death any of our people who ventured to approach the coasts of Europe.

But that is only part of the story. We know now as clearly as we knew before we were ourselves engaged that we are not the enemies of the German people and that they are not our enemies. They did not originate or desire this hideous war or wish that we should be drawn into it; and we are vaguely conscious that we are fighting their cause, as they will some day see it, as well as our own.

They are themselves in the grip of the same sinister power that has now at last stretched its ugly talons out and drawn blood from us. The whole world is at war because the whole world is in the grip of that power and is trying out the great battle which shall determine whether it is to be brought under its mastery or fling itself free.

For us there is but one choice. We have made it. Woe be to the man or group of men that seeks to stand in our way in this day of high resolution, when every principle we hold dearest is to be vindicated and made secure for the salvation of the nations. We are ready to plead at the bar of history, and our flag shall wear a new luster. Once more we shall make good with our lives and fortunes the great faith to which we were born, and a new glory shall shine in the face of our people.

THE STAR-SPANGLED BANNER
FRANCIS SCOTT KEY

Oh, say, can you see, by the dawn's early light,
   What so proudly we hail'd at the twilight's last gleaming,
Whose broad stripes and bright stars, thro' the perilous fight,
   O'er the ramparts we watch'd, were so gallantly streaming?

And the rocket's red glare, the bombs bursting in air,
Gave proof thro' the night that our flag was still there.
   Oh, say, does that star-spangled banner yet wave
    O'er the land of the free and the home of the brave?

On the shore dimly seen through the mist of the deep,
   Where the foe's haughty host in dread silence reposes,
What is that which the breeze, o'er the towering steep,
   As it fitfully blows, half conceals, half discloses?
Now it catches the gleam of the morning's first beam,
In full glory reflected, now shines on the stream:
   'T is the star-spangled banner! oh, long may it wave
    O'er the land of the free and the home of the brave!

And where is that band who so vauntingly swore,
   That the havoc of war and the battle's confusion,
A home and a country should leave us no more?
   Their blood has washed out their foul footsteps' pollution.
No refuge could save the hireling and slave
From the terror of flight or the gloom of the grave:
   And the star-spangled banner in triumph doth wave
    O'er the land of the free and the home of the brave.

Oh, thus be it ever when freemen shall stand
   Between their loved homes and wild war's desolation;
Blest with victory and peace, may the heaven-rescued land
   Praise the Power that hath made and preserved us a nation!
Then conquer we must, when our cause it is just,
And this be our motto: "In God is our trust."
   And the star-spangled banner in triumph shall wave
    O'er the land of the free and the home of the brave.

MAKERS OF THE FLAG
FRANKLIN K. LANE

This morning, as I passed into the Land Office, The Flag dropped me a most cordial salutation, and from its rippling folds I heard it say: "Good morning, Mr. Flag Maker."

"I beg your pardon, Old Glory," I said, "aren't you mistaken? I am not the President of the United States, nor a member of Congress, nor even a general in the army. I am only a Government clerk."

"I greet you again, Mr. Flag Maker," replied the gay voice. "I know you well. You are the man who worked in the swelter of yesterday straightening out the tangle of that farmer's homestead in Idaho, or perhaps you found the mistake in that Indian contract in Oklahoma, or helped to clear that patent for the hopeful inventor in New York, or pushed the opening of that new ditch in Colorado, or made that mine in Illinois more safe, or brought relief to the old soldier in Wyoming. No matter; whichever one of these beneficent individuals you may happen to be, I give you greeting, Mr. Flag Maker."

I was about to pass on, when The Flag stopped me with these words:

"Yesterday the President spoke a word that made happier the future of ten million peons in Mexico; but that act looms no larger on the flag than the struggle which the boy in Georgia is making to win the Corn Club prize this summer.

"Yesterday the Congress spoke a word which will open the door of Alaska; but a mother in Michigan worked from sunrise until far into the night, to give her boy an education. She, too, is making the flag.

FRANKLIN K. LANE

MAKERS OF THE FLAG

"Yesterday we made a new law to prevent financial panics, and yesterday, maybe, a school teacher in Ohio taught his first letters to a boy who will one day write a song that will give cheer to the millions of our race. We are all making the flag."

"But," I said impatiently, "these people were only working!"

Then came a great shout from The Flag:

"The work that we do is the making of the flag.

"I am not the flag; not at all. I am but its shadow.

"I am whatever you make me, nothing more.

"I am your belief in yourself, your dream of what a People may become.

"I live a changing life, a life of moods and passions, of heartbreaks and tired muscles.

"Sometimes I am strong with pride, when men do an honest work, fitting the rails together truly.

"Sometimes I droop, for then purpose has gone from me, and cynically I play the coward.

"Sometimes I am loud, garish, and full of that ego that blasts judgment.

"But always, I am all that you hope to be, and have the courage to try for.

"I am song and fear, struggle and panic, and ennobling hope.

"I am the day's work of the weakest man, and the largest dream of the most daring.

"I am the Constitution and the courts, statutes and the statute makers, soldier and dreadnaught, drayman and street sweep, cook, counselor, and clerk.

"I am the battle of yesterday, and the mistake of tomorrow.

"I am the mystery of the men who do without knowing why.

"I am the clutch of an idea, and the reasoned purpose of resolution.

"I am no more than what you believe me to be and I am all that you believe I can be.

"I am what you make me, nothing more.

"I swing before your eyes as a bright gleam of color, a symbol of yourself, the pictured suggestion of that big thing which makes this nation. My stars and my stripes are your dream and your labors. They are bright with cheer, brilliant with courage, firm with faith, because you have made them so out of your hearts. For you are the makers of the flag and it is well that you glory in the making."

THE FLAG
EDITH M. THOMAS

I walked at noon down Broadway,
And east I turned at Wall,
Crossed Nassau Street and William —
Old Glory over all! —
Did you not do the same to-day —
And brush the sudden tear away?

The hanging gardens — how they bloom
Far up the builded canyon's gloom!
There never was before a spring
Of such a wondrous blossoming
To make the eye and heart adore! . . .
  How beautiful, how beautiful —
How beautiful I never knew before!

The hanging gardens — Oh, how brave
When on the lifting wind they wave!
Nor flaw nor frost can work them wrong,
Perennial is the stock, and strong —
In hardihood 't was sown of yore! . . .
   How beautiful, how beautiful —
How beautiful I never knew before!

The hanging gardens — colors three
Are all the raptured eye can see.
No flower exotic here has place,
But all are sprung of native race —
The red, the white, the blue — not more . . .
   How beautiful, how beautiful —
How beautiful I never knew before!

The hanging gardens — and how far
May crimson band and candid star
A looming throw in other skies
O'er lands where kindred blooms shall rise
From broadcast seed that Freedom bore . . .
   How beautiful, how beautiful —
How beautiful I never knew before!

FOLLOW THE FLAG
THEODORE MARBURG

Follow the flag!

By every fireside where live the love of country and the love of justice is heard a sigh of relief that our flag is not, after all, to be trampled in the mire. Now that it has been **raised** aloft. follow it. Follow it even to the battle front.

Follow the flag!

It goes on a *high* mission. The land over which it flies inherited its spirit of freedom from a race which had practiced liberty for a thousand years. And the daughter paid back the debt to the mother. Her successful practice of free institutions caused the civic stature of the citizen in the mother-land to grow. It lit the torch of liberty in France. Then, moving abreast, these three lands of democracy imparted to it impetus so resistless that freedom is sweeping victorious around the globe. To-day constitutional government is the rule, not the exception, in the world. Once more these three nations are together leading a great cause and this time as brothers in arms.

Follow the flag!

It goes on a *world* mission. If the high hope of our President is fulfilled, that flag will have new meaning. Just as the stars and stripes in it symbolized the union of free states in America, so now they may come to symbolize the beginnings of a union of nations, self-governing, and, because they are self-governing, making for good will and for justice.

Follow the flag!

It goes on a *stern* mission. Follow it, not for revenge, yet in anger—righteous anger against the bloody crew who, with criminal intent, have brought upon the world the greatest sum of human misery it has ever known in all its history. Follow it till that ugly company is put down and the very people themselves whom they have so grievously deceived and misled, by coming into liberty, will come to bless that flag and kiss its gleaming folds.

Follow the flag!

Too long it has been absent from that line in France where once again an Attila has been stopped. It has been needed there, God knows! And yet, though not visible to the eye, it is and has been there from the beginning. It is there in the hearts of those fifty thousand American boys who saw their duty clear and moved up to it. Now at last it may be flung to the breeze in the front line, to be visible by day, and to remain at nightfall, like the blessings of a prayer fulfilled, in the consciousness of men. Follow it and take your stand beside the fifty thousand.

Follow the flag!

THE KID HAS GONE TO THE COLORS
W. M. HERSCHELL

The Kid has gone to the Colors
And we don't know what to say;
The Kid we have loved and cuddled
Stepped out for the Flag to-day.
We thought him a child, a baby,
With never a care at all,
But his country called him man-size,
And the Kid has heard the call.

He paused to watch the recruiting,
Where, fired by the fife and drum,
He bowed his head to Old Glory
And thought that it whispered: "Come!"

THE SPIRIT OF DEMOCRACY

The Kid, not being a slacker,
Stood forth with patriot-joy
To add his name to the roster—
And God, we're proud of the boy!

The Kid has gone to the Colors;
It seems but a little while
Since he drilled a school boy army
In a truly martial style.
But now he's a man, a soldier,
And we lend him listening ear,
For his heart is a heart all loyal,
Unscourged by the curse of fear.

His dad, when he told him, shuddered;
His mother—God bless her!—cried;
Yet, blest with a mother-nature,
She wept with a mother-pride.
But he whose old shoulders straightened
Was Granddad—for memory ran
To years when he, too, a youngster,
Was changed by the Flag to a man!

PUTTING THE FLAG ON THE FIRING LINE [1]
THEODORE ROOSEVELT

I come here tonight to appeal to the people of the great west, the people of the Mississippi valley, the people who are the spiritual heirs of the men who stood behind Lincoln and Grant.

You men and women who live beside the Great Lakes and on the lands drained by the Ohio, the Mississippi, and the Missouri have always represented what is most intensely American in our national life. When once waked up to actual conditions you have always stood with unfaltering courage and iron endurance for the national honor and the national interest.

I appeal to the sons and daughters of the men and women of the Civil War, to the grandsons and granddaughters of the pioneers; I appeal to the women as much as to the men, for our nation has risen level to every great crisis only because in every such crisis the courage of its women flamed as high as the courage of the men.

I appeal to you to take the lead in making good the President's message, in which he set forth the reasons why it was our unescapable duty to make war upon Germany. It rests with us — with the American people — to make that message one of the great state documents of our history.

Then let us steel our hearts and gird our loins to show that we are fit to stand among the free people whose freedom is buttressed by their self-reliant strength. Let us show by our deeds that we are fit to be the heirs of the

---
[1] From the speech delivered in Chicago, April 28, 1917.

men who founded the republic, and of the men who saved the republic; of the continentals who followed Washington, and of the men who wore the blue under Grant and the gray under Lee.

But, mind you, the message, the speech, will amount to nothing unless we make it good; and it can be made good only by the high valor of our fighting men, and by the resourceful and laborious energy of the men and women who, with deeds, not merely words, back up the fighting men.

We read the Declaration of Independence every Fourth of July because—and only because—the soldiers of Washington made that message good by their blood during the weary years of war that followed. If, after writing the Declaration of Independence, the men of '76 had failed with their bodies to make it good, it would be read now only with contempt and derision.

Our children still learn how Patrick Henry spoke for the heart of the American people when he said, "Give me liberty or give me death," but this generation is thrilled by his words only because the Americans of those days showed in very fact that they were ready to accept death rather than lose their liberty.

In Lincoln's deathless Gettysburg speech and second inaugural he solemnly pledged the honor of the American people to the hard and perilous task of preserving the union and freeing the slaves.

The pledge was kept. The American people fought to a finish the war which saved the union and freed the slave. If Lincoln and the men and women behind him had wavered, if they had grown fainthearted and had shrunk from the fight, or had merely paid others to fight for them, they would have earned for themselves and for us the scorn of the nations of mankind.

The words of Lincoln will live forever only because they were made good by the deeds of the fighting men.

So it is now. We can make the President's message of April 2nd stand among the great state papers in our history; but we can do so only if we make the message good; and we can make it good only if we fight with all our strength now, at once; if at the earliest possible moment we put the flag on the firing line and keep it there, over a constantly growing army, until the war closes by a peace which brings victory to the great cause of democracy and civilization, the great cause of justice and fair play among the peoples of the world.

FAME'S TRUE APPLAUSE
GEORGE EDWARD WOODBERRY

It cannot be that men who are the seed
    Of Washington should miss fame's true applause:
    Franklin did plan us; Marshall gave us laws;
And slow the broad scroll grew a people's creed,—
One land and free! then at our dangerous need,
    Time's challenge coming, Lincoln gave it pause,
    Upheld the double pillars of the cause,
And dying left them whole,— the crowning deed.

Such was the fathering race that made all fast,
    Who founded us, and spread from sea to sea,
    A thousand leagues, the zone of liberty,
And built for man this refuge from his past,
    Unkinged, unchurched, unsoldiered; shamed were we,
Failing the stature that such sires forecast.

STAND BY THE FLAG

Stand by the flag, its folds have streamed in glory,
  To foes a fear, to friends a festal robe,
And spread in rhythmic lines the sacred story
  Of freedom's triumphs over all the globe;
Stand by the flag, on land, and ocean billow;
  By it your fathers stood, unmoved and true:
Living, defended; dying, from their pillow,
  With their last blessing, pass'd it on to you.

Stand by the flag, though death shots round it rattle
  And underneath its waving folds have met,
In all the dread array of sanguine battle,
  The quivering lance and glittering bayonet;
Stand by the flag, all doubt and treason scorning,
  Believe, with courage firm and faith sublime,
That it will float until the eternal morning
  Pales in its glories all the lights of time.

THE CALL TO BATTLE

GILBERT SHELDON

If through the dust of conflict thou descry
    The shining of the standard of the Lord,
    Do thou arise and buckle on thy sword,
And follow where it leads undoubtingly.

Thou hast the Light: see that thou walk thereby!
    Exceeding great and sure is his reward
    Whose purpose with his vision doth accord,
And as his soul speaks so his acts reply.

THE CALL TO BATTLE

And if it shall be told thee that the foe
    Beholds the banner that thou deemst thine own
    March in his van to battle, be not wroth.
The truth is other than the truths we know;
    His cause and thine are laid before the throne,
    And God inclines to neither and to both.

—From *The Nation*

THE WORLD SIGNIFICANCE OF THE WAR
WILLIAM HOWARD TAFT

England, France, Russia, Italy, and now the United States, as allies, are engaged in the greatest war of history to secure permanent world peace. With twenty or more millions of men at the colors, with losses in dead, wounded and captured of more than twenty-five per cent, with debts piling mountain-high and reaching many, many billions, they are fighting for a definite purpose, and that is the defeat of German militarism.

If the Prussian military caste retains its power to control the military and foreign policy of Germany after the war, peace will not be permanent, and war will begin again when the chauvinistic advisers of the Hohenzollern dynasty deem a conquest and victory possible.

The Allies have made a stupendous effort and have strained their utmost capacity. Unready for the war, they have concentrated their energy in preparation. In this important respect they have defeated the plan of Germany "in shining armor" to crush her enemies in their unreadiness.

But the war has not been won. Germany is in possession of Belgium and part of northern France. She holds Serbia and Rumania, Poland and the Baltic Provinces of Russia. Peace now, even though it be made on the basis of the restoration of the *status quo*, "without indemnities and without annexations," would be a failure to achieve the great purpose for which the Allies have made heart-rending sacrifice. Armaments would continue for the

WILLIAM HOWARD TAFT

next war, and this war would have been fought in vain. The millions of lives lost and the hundreds of billions' worth of the product of men's labor would be wasted.

He who proposes peace now, therefore, either does not see the stake for which the Allies are fighting, or wishes the German military autocracy still to control the destinies of all of us as to peace or war. Those who favor permanent world peace must oppose with might and main the proposals for peace at this juncture in the war.

The Allies are fighting for a principle the maintenance of which affects the future of civilization. If they do not achieve it they have sacrificed the flower of their youth and mortgaged their future for a century, and all for nothing.

This is not a war in which the stake is territory or the sphere of influence of one nation over another. The Allies cannot concede peace until they conquer it. When they do so, it will be permanent. Otherwise they fail.

There are wars like that between Japan and Russia, in which President Roosevelt properly and successfully intervened to bring about peace that helped the parties to a settlement. The principle at stake and the power and territory were of such a character that a settlement might be made substantially permanent. But the present issue is like that in our Civil War, which was whether the Union was to be preserved and the cancer of slavery was to be cut out. Peace proposals to President Lincoln were quite as numerous as those of to-day, and were moved by quite as high motives. But there was no compromise possible. Slavery and disunion either lost or won. So to-day the great moral object of the war must be achieved or defeated.

TOGETHER

ALFRED AUSTIN

Who say we cherish far-off feud,
   Still nurse the ancient grudges?
Show me the title of this brood
   Of self-appointed judges;
Their name, their race, their nation, clan,
   And we will teach them whether
We do not, as none others can,
   Feel, think, and work together!

Both speak the tongue that Milton spoke,
   Shakespeare and Chatham wielded,
And Washington and all his folk
   When their just claim was yielded.
In it both lisp, both learn, both pray,
   Dirge death, and thus the tether
Grows tighter, tenderer, every day,
   That binds the two together.

Our ways are one, and one our aim,
   And one will be our story,
Who fight for Freedom, not for fame,
   From Duty, not for glory;
Both stock of the old Home, where blow
   Shamrock, and rose, and heather,
And every year link arms and go
   Through its loved haunts together.

Should envious aliens plan and plot
   'Gainst one and now the other,
They swift would learn how strong the knot
   Binds brother unto brother.
How quickly they would change their tack

And show the recreant feather,
Should Star-and-Stripe and Union Jack
But float mast-high together.

Now let us give one hearty grip,
　As by true men is given,
And vow eternal fellowship
　That never shall be riven;
And with our peaceful flags unfurled,
　Be fair or foul the weather,
Should need arise, face all the world,
　And stand or fall together.

PEACE
ELIZABETH BARRETT BROWNING

I love no peace which is not fellowship
　And which includes not mercy. I would have
Rather the raking of the guns across
　The world, and shrieks against Heaven's architrave . . .

Such things are better than a Peace that sits
　Beside a hearth in self-commended mood,
And takes no thought how wind and rain by fits
　Are howling out of doors against the good
Of the poor wanderer. What! Your peace admits
　Of outside anguish while it keeps at home?
I loathe to take its name upon my tongue.
　'T is nowise peace: 't is treason, stiff with doom —
This gagged despair and inarticulate wrong. . . .

O Lord of Peace, who art Lord of Righteousness,
　Constrain the anguished worlds from sin and grief,
Pierce them with conscience, purge them with redress,
　And give us peace which is no counterfeit!

THE CALL OF THE REPUBLIC
GEORGE HAVEN PUTNAM

The Government is our Government. We have made it. The President represents the votes of a majority of his fellow citizens. The Congressmen are the men we have selected for our national councils. We ourselves are responsible for the policy of the Republic. We owe it to ourselves as well as to the State to repress with promptness all injustice and to maintain law and order.

The Germany I knew as a student, the good old Germany, the Germany of ideals, for which Germany fought in 1848 — the ideals of Goethe, Lessing, Körner, Richter, and other thinkers and fighters for freedom—has been poisoned by the fumes of prussic acid from Berlin. One result of this war must be to cleanse Germany from this Prussian poison.

We came into this war very late. Our responsibility is therefore graver. Under the pressure of war our people have been brought together. We see the evolution of a nation's soul. We go into this war with Lincoln's motto: "Let us have faith that right makes might and in that faith let us do our duty as we understand it."

The world's war has now resolved itself into an issue of will power. The people who are fighting for the liberty of the world must be able to show an assured purpose and conviction and to back up that conviction with action in such fashion that the forces which have attempted to secure the domination of Europe and the world shall be driven back. It is clear that they have already failed in their original purpose. They must be so overcome that

GEORGE HAVEN PUTNAM

a repetition of a war of aggression shall be impossible. This struggle is a war against war, and it must be so continued that we shall have at the completion an assured peace, a peace with justice, a peace that will maintain throughout the world the right of men to life, liberty, and the pursuit of happiness.

THE BUILDING OF THE SHIP
HENRY W. LONGFELLOW

* * * * *

Thou, too, sail on, O Ship of State!
Sail on, O UNION, strong and great!
Humanity with all its fears,
With all the hopes of future years,
Is hanging breathless on thy fate!
We know what Master laid thy keel,
What Workmen wrought thy ribs of steel,
Who made each mast, and sail, and rope,
What anvils rang, what hammers beat,
In what a forge and what a heat
Were shaped the anchors of thy hope!
Fear not each sudden sound and shock,
'T is of the wave and not the rock;
'T is but the flapping of the sail,
And not a rent made by the gale!
In spite of rock and tempest's roar,
In spite of false lights on the shore,
Sail on, nor fear to breast the sea!
Our hearts, our hopes, are all with thee,
Our hearts, our hopes, our prayers, our tears,
Our faith triumphant o'er our fears,
Are all with thee — are all with thee!

IT IS TIME

It is time! Come, all together, come!
Not to the fife's call, not to the drum;
Right needs you; Truth claims you —
That's a call indeed
One must heed!
Not for the weeping
(God knows there is weeping!);
Not for the horrors
That are blotting out the page;
Not for our comrades
(How many now are sleeping!)
Nor for the pity nor the rage,
But for the sake of simple goodness
And His laws,
We shall sacrifice our all
For The Cause!

—From Lloyd Roberts' "Come Quietly, Britain

A SIMPLE SONG FOR AMERICA

KARLE WILSON BAKER

Gather us to thy heart,
  Lay us thy spirit bare:
Give us in thee our part,
  O Mother young and fair!

Thou art so great, so great,
  Thy children are so small,
We cannot guess thy state
  Nor compass thee at all.

A SIMPLE SONG FOR AMERICA

Our spirits yearn and ache
  To forge from these few years,
What soberer peoples make
  From centuries of tears:

Love, like a tempered sword,
  Glittering forth at need!
We can but pray the Lord
  Who knows nor church nor creed,

The Day-spring from above,
  The Truth that maketh free:
Give us great hearts to love
  A great land worthily!

OUR MORAL LEADERSHIP[1]
EDMUND J JAMES

We are gathered here, not so much to review what we have done or failed to do in the Great War during the past year, as to dedicate ourselves anew to the great enterprise that we have undertaken.

In spite of all that has been said during the year in which we have been at war with the Central Powers of Europe, sustaining and helping our hard-pressed and courageous Allies, it does not seem to me that the average American citizen even yet realizes what a fundamental world issue is involved; how great is our privilege in being permitted to enter this conflict actively and on the right side; how important a turning point in the history of the world the outcome of this war may be; and how fortunate we are in having a president who has seized the opportunity to convert what to a narrow observer seemed a mere struggle for additional territory and additional material resources into a great issue in the progress of human freedom.

When Louis XVI called together the Estates General in the year 1789 to take counsel as to the state of the kingdom, a struggle arose between the king and the representatives of the various orders, which might easily have remained a mere local incident in the life of a single nation. But the genius of the French people converted it into a great crusade for liberty, equality, and fraternity, out of which grew that mighty convulsion, called simply

[1] From the speech delivered April, 1918.

Edmund Janes James

"The Revolution," so fundamental in its characteristics and results, so sweeping in its wide-spread influence, that all previous human history seemed a mere preparation for it and all subsequent history a mere outcome of it; all previous lines of development seeming to converge toward it and all subsequent lines of progress to spring out of it.

The present war at first was regarded by some as a mere contest on the part of great nations for more territory and a larger population and greater wealth. It was natural to judge from previous human experiences that smaller powers standing in the way of the waves of this furious struggle for national supremacy would be swept away, devastated, ruined, utterly effaced perhaps — and that all this would happen as so inevitably a result of the conflict of great powers that while much sympathy might be felt or even expressed, the only active result would be a shrugging of the shoulders and an "alas! alas! Such is life. Such is the fate of the small man! and the small nation!"

And then the conduct of the Central Powers became such that even those Americans who did not appreciate or care for a moral role among the nations for the Great Republic saw themselves constrained to force action in order to defend our national independence, nay, our national existence.

Even then the issue might have been narrowed and might have been formulated as a selfish one, affecting ourselves alone or the particular desires of national units, such as the securing to Italy of the territory it desired at the expense of Austria, or the giving to Russia of the right to determine the eastern boundaries of Germany, while to France and England should be given a similar privilege as to the western boundaries, and the assignment to England of the German Colonies — a kind of dispute in which the American people could have little personal interest except so far as it safeguarded or threatened our power or security.

With one noble and sweeping gesture President Wilson wiped out all these items on the slate of world division and organization and wrote down as our goal the safeguarding of human liberty throughout the earth: to all people — not merely to ourselves — to the small as well as to the great — to the weak as well as to the strong — the assurance that they may order their own lives as freemen.

The stars in their courses are fighting for us and our cause, and if only we are true to the high ideals we have adopted, and show ourselves worthy of our ancestry — in energy, in perseverance, in skill, and in devotion — the victory, an overwhelming victory will be ours.

A victory for us means victory for the forces of righteousness and of progress; protection for the small nation and the small man, for women and children. It means LIBERTY and FREEDOM for all!

"OH MOTHER OF A MIGHTY RACE"

WILLIAM CULLEN BRYANT

Ay, let them rail — those haughty ones,
While safe thou dwellest with thy sons.
They do not know how loved thou art,
How many a fond and fearless heart
    Would rise to throw
Its life between thee and the foe.

"OH MOTHER OF A MIGHTY RACE"

They know not, in their hate and pride,
What virtues with thy children bide;
How true, how good, thy graceful maids
Make bright, like flowers, the valley-shades;
    What generous men
Spring, like thine oaks, by hill and glen;—

What cordial welcomes greet the guest
By thy lone rivers of the West;
How faith is kept, and truth revered,
And man is loved and God is feared,
    In woodland homes,
And where the ocean border foams.

There's freedom at thy gates, and rest
For earth's down-trodden and opprest,
A shelter for the hunted head,
For the starved laborer toil and bread.
    Power, at thy bounds,
Stops and calls back his baffled hounds.

Oh, fair young mother! on thy brow
Shall sit a nobler grace than now.
Deep in the brightness of the skies
The thronging years in glory rise,
    And, as they fleet,
Drop strength and riches at thy feet.

ON PATROL

He went to sea on the long patrol,
Away to the East from the Corton Shoal,
    But now he's overdue.
He signaled me as he bore away
A flickering lamp through leaping spray,
And darkness then till judgment day,
    "So long! Good luck to you!"

He's waiting out on the long patrol,
Till the names are called at the muster-roll
    Of seamen overdue.
Far above him, in wind and rain,
Another is on patrol again —
The gap is closed in the Naval Chain
    Where all the links are new.

Over his head the seas are white,
And the wind is blowing a gale to-night,
    As if the Storm-King knew,
And roared a ballad of sleet and snow
To the man that lies on the sand below,
A trumpet-song for the winds to blow
    To seamen overdue.

Was it sudden or slow — the death that came?
Roaring water or sheets of flame?
    The end with none to view?
No man can tell us the way he died,
But over the clouds Valkyries ride
To open the gates and hold them wide
    For seamen overdue.

But whether the end was swift or slow,
By the Hand of God, or a German blow,
  My messmate overdue —
You went to Death — and the whisper ran
As over the Gates the horns began
Splendor of God! We have found a man.
  Goodbye! Good luck to you!

—From *Blackwood's Magazine*

ENGLAND UNSHEATHES THE SWORD [1]
HERBERT H. ASQUITH

My Lord Mayor and Citizens of London:

It is three and a half years since I last had the honor of addressing in this hall a gathering of the citizens. We were then met under the Presidency of one of your predecessors, men of all creeds and parties, to celebrate and approve the joint declaration of the two great English-speaking States that for the future any differences between them should be settled, if not by agreement, at least by judicial inquiry and arbitration, and never in any circumstances by war. Those of us who hailed that great Eirenicon between the United States and ourselves as a landmark on the road of progress were not sanguine enough to think, or even to hope, that the era of war was drawing to a close. . But still less were we prepared to anticipate the terrible spectacle which now confronts us of a contest which for the number and importance of the powers engaged, the scale of their armaments and armies, the width of the theater of conflict, the outpouring of blood and the loss of life, the incalculable toll of suffering levied upon non-combatants, the material and moral loss accumulating day by day to the higher interests of civilized mankind — a contest which in every one of these aspects is without precedent in the annals of the world. We were very confident three years ago in the rightness of our position, when we welcomed the new securities for peace. We are equally confident in it today, when reluctantly, and against our will, but with a clear judgment

---
[1] Delivered September 5, 1914.

and a clean conscience we find ourselves involved with the whole strength of this empire in a bloody arbitration between might and right. The issue has passed out of the domain of argument into another field, but let me ask you, and through you the world outside, what would have been our condition as a nation today if we had been base enough through timidity or through perverted calculation of self-interest, or through a paralysis of the sense of honor and duty, if we had been base enough to be false to our word and faithless to our friends?

Our eyes would have been turned at this moment with those of the whole civilized world to Belgium, a small State, which has lived for more than seventy years under the several and collective guarantee to which we in common with Prussia and Austria were parties, and we should have seen at the instance and by the action of two of these guaranteeing powers her neutrality violated, her independence strangled, her territory made use of as affording the easiest and the most convenient road to a war of unprovoked aggression against France. We, the British people, would at this moment have been standing by with folded arms and with such countenance as we could command while this small and unprotected State, in defense of her vital liberties, made a heroic stand against overweening and overwhelming force; we should have been admiring as detached spectators the siege of Liège, the steady and manful resistance of a small army to the occupation of their capital, with its splendid traditions and memories, the gradual forcing back of the patriotic defenders of their native land to the ramparts of Antwerp, countless outrages inflicted by buccaneering levies exacted from the unoffending civil population, and, finally, the greatest crime committed against civilization and culture since the Thirty Years' War, the sack of Louvain, with its buildings, its pictures, its unique library, its unrivaled associations — a shameless holocaust of priceless treasures lit by blind barbarian vengeance. What account should we, the Government and the people of this country, have been able to render to the tribunal of our national conscience and sense of honor, if, in defiance of our plighted and solemn obligations, we had endured, nay, if we had not done our best to prevent, yes, and to avenge these intolerable outrages? For my part I say that sooner than be a silent witness — which means in effect a willing accomplice — of this tragic triumph of force over law and of brutality over freedom, I would see this country of ours blotted out of the pages of history.

THE CALL
R. E. VERNÈDE

Lad, with the merry smile and the eyes
    Quick as a hawk's and clear as the day,
You, who have counted the game the prize,
    Here is the game of games to play.
Never a goal — the captains say —
Matches the one that's needed now:
    Put the old blazer and cap away —
England's colors await your brow.

Man, with the square-set jaws and chin,
    Always, it seems, you have moved to your end
Sure of yourself, intent to win
    Fame and wealth and the power to bend.

THE CALL

All that you've made you're called to spend,
All that you've sought you're asked to miss;
  What's ambition compared with this —
That a man lay down his life for his friend?

Dreamer, oft in your glancing mind
  Brave with drinking the faerie brew,
You have smitten the ogres blind
  When the fair Princess cried out to you.
  Dreamer, what if your dreams are true?
Yonder's a bayonet, magical, since
  Him whom it strikes, the blade sinks through —
Take it and strike for England, Prince!

Friend with the face so hard and worn,
  The Devil and you have sometime met,
And now you curse the day you were born
  And want one boon of God — to forget.
  Ah, but I know, and yet — and yet —
I think, out there in the shrapnel spray,
  You shall stand up and not regret
The Life that gave so splendid a day.

Lover of ease, you've lolled and forgot
  All the things that you meant to right;
Life has been soft for you, has it not?
  What offer does England make to-night?
  This — to toil and to march and to fight
As never you've dreamed since your life began;
  This — to carry the steel-swept height,
This — to know that you've played the man!

Brothers, brothers, the time is short,
  Nor soon again shall it so betide
That a man may pass from the common sort
  Sudden and stand by the heroes' side.
    Are there some that being named yet bide?
Hark once more to the clarion call —
  Sounded by him who deathless died —
"This day England expects you all."

AN INVOCATION
BEATRICE BARRY

That little children may in safety ride
  The strong, clean waters of Thy splendid seas;
That Anti-Christ be no more glorified,
  Nor mock Thy justice with his blasphemies,
We come, but not with threats or braggart boasts
  Hear us, Lord God of Hosts!

That Liberty be not betrayed and sold,
  And that her sons prove worthy of the breed;
That Freedom's flag may shelter as of old,
  Nor decorate the shrines of Gold and Greed,
We come; and on our consecrated sword
  We ask Thy blessing, Lord.

That honor be among those priceless things
  Without which life shall seem of little worth:
That covenants be not the sport of kings;
  That freedom shall not perish from the earth,
We come; across a scarred and bloodstained sod
  Lead us, Almighty God!

THE SPIRES OF OXFORD
WINIFRED M. LETTS

I saw the spires of Oxford
　As I was passing by,
The gray spires of Oxford
　Against the pearl-gray sky.
My heart was with the Oxford men
　Who went abroad to die.

The years go fast in Oxford,
　The golden years and gay,
The hoary Colleges look down
　On careless boys at play.
But when the bugles sounded war
　They put their games away.

They left the peaceful river,
　The cricket-field, the quad,
The shaven lawns of Oxford,
　To seek a bloody sod—
They gave their merry youth away
　For country and for God.

God rest you, happy gentlemen,
　Who laid your good lives down,
Who took the khaki and the gun
　Instead of cap and gown.
God bring you a fairer place
　Than even Oxford town.

TO THE ARMY!

Soldiers:

Without the least provocation on our part, a neighbor, glorying in his power, has torn into shreds the treaties that bear his signature and violated the territory of our fathers.

Because we have been worthy of ourselves, because we have refused to forfeit our honor, he has attacked us. But the whole world is amazed at our loyal stand. May its respect and its esteem sustain you in this supreme moment!

Seeing its freedom menaced, the nation has been deeply moved and her children have hurried to her frontiers. Valiant soldiers of a sacred cause, I have confidence in your tenacious bravery, and I salute you in the name of Belgium. Your citizens are proud of you. You will triumph, for yours is the might that serves the right.

Cæsar said of your ancestors: "Of all the peoples of Gaul the Belgians are the bravest."

Hail to you, army of the Belgian people! In the face of the enemy, remember that you are fighting for liberty and for your menaced hearths. Remember, men of Flanders, the Battle of the Golden Spurs; and you, Wallons, who now stand on your honor, remember the six hundred Franchimontois.

Soldiers! I leave Brussels to put myself at your head.

ALBERT.

Done at the Palace of Brussels, this fifth day of August, 1914.

KING ALBERT

Shy and smiling midst his soldiers
Like some young father 'mongst big sons,
In the cold and through the gloom,
The King moves along the trenches
Speaking little, quietly and slow:
"Patience, all is well, work on!"
A handclasp and a look, then he is gone
And those who could not see his face
Take comfort that they heard his passing step.
—From Emile Cammaerts' "The King and the Emperor"

THE PRAYER
AMELIA JOSEPHINE BURR
[The real experience of a French gunner]

You say there's only evil in this war —
That bullets drive out Christ? If you had been
In Furnes with me that night — what would you say,
I wonder?
              It was ruin past all words,
Horror where joyous comfort used to be,
And not clean quiet death, for all day long
The great shells tore the little that remained
Like vultures on a body that still breathes.
They stopped as it grew dark. I looked about
The ghastly wilderness that once had been
The village street, and saw no other life
Except a Belgian soldier, shadowy
Among the shadows, and a little group
Of children creeping from a cellar school
And hurrying home. One older than the rest —
So little older! — mothered them along

Till all at once a stray belated shell
Whined suddenly out of the gloom, and burst
Near by. The babies wailed and clung together,
Helpless with fear. In vain the little mother
Encouraged them—"But no! You mustn't cry,
That isn't brave, that isn't French!" At last
She led her frightened brood across the way
To where there stood a roadside Calvary
Bearing its sad, indomitable Christ —
Strange how the shells will spare just that! I saw
So many . . . There they knelt, poor innocents,
Hands folded and eyes closed. I stole across
And stood behind them. "We must say our prayer
Our Father which art in heaven," she began,
And all the little sobbing voices piped,
"Hallowed be Thy Name." From down the road
The Belgian soldier had come near. I felt
Him standing there beside me in the dusk.
"Thy kingdom come —"
                        "Thy will be done on earth
As it is in heaven." The irony of it
Cut me like steel. I barely kept an oath
Behind my teeth. If one could name this earth
In the same breath with heaven — what is hell?
Only a little child could pray like this.
"Give us this day our daily bread —" A pause.
There was no answer. She repeated it
Urgently. Still the hush. She opened wide
Reproachful eyes at them. Their eyes were open
Also, and staring at the shadowy shapes
Of ruin all around them. Now that prayer
Had grown too hard even for little children.

"I know — I know — but we *must* say the prayer,"
She faltered. "Give us this day our daily bread,
And — and forgive —" she stopped.
                             "Our trespasses
As we forgive them who have trespassed against us."
The children turned amazed, to see who spoke
The words they could not. I too turned to him,
The soldier there beside me — and I looked
Into King Albert's face . . . I have no words
To tell you what I saw . . . only I thought
That while a man's breast holds a heart like that,
Christ was not — even here — so far away.

IN FLANDERS FIELDS
JOHN McCRAE

In Flanders fields the poppies blow
Between the crosses, row on row,
    That mark our place, and in the sky,
    The larks, still bravely singing, fly,
Scarce heard amid the guns below.

We are the dead; short days ago
We lived, felt dawn, saw sunset glow,
    Loved and were loved, and now we lie
        In Flanders fields.

Take up our quarrel with the foe!
To you from failing hands we throw
    The torch; be yours to hold it high!
    If ye break faith with us who die
We shall not sleep, though poppies grow
        In Flanders fields.

                                      —From *Punch*

BELGIUM SHALL RISE[1]
CARDINAL MERCIER

My dearest brethren, I desire to utter, in your name and my own, the gratitude of those whose age, vocation, and social conditions cause them to benefit by the heroism of others, without bearing in it any active part.

If any man had rescued you from shipwreck or from fire, you would assuredly hold yourselves bound to him by a debt of everlasting thankfulness. But it is not one man, it is two hundred and fifty thousand men, who fought, who suffered, who fell for you, so that Belgium might keep her independence, her dynasty, her patriotic unity; so that after the vicissitudes of battle she might rise nobler, purer, more erect, and more glorious than before.

In your name I sent them the greeting of our fraternal sympathy and our assurance that not only do we pray for the success of their arms and for the eternal welfare of their souls, but that we also accept for their sake all the distress, whether physical or moral, that falls to our own share in the oppression that hourly besets us, and all that the future may have in store for us, in humiliation for a time, in anxiety, and in sorrow. In the days of final victory we shall be in honor; it is just that today we should all be in grief.

Oh, all too easily do I understand how natural instinct rebels against the evils that have fallen upon Belgium; the spontaneous thought of mankind is ever that virtue should have its instantaneous crown, and injustice its immediate retribution. But the ways of God are not our

---
[1] Extract from the famous pastoral letter of Cardinal Mercier, December 25, 1914.

CARDINAL MERCIER

CARDINAL MANNING

ways. Providence gives free way, for a time measured by divine wisdom, to human passions and the conflict of desires. God, being eternal, is patient. The last word is the word of mercy, and it belongs to those who believe in love.

Better than any other man, perhaps, do I know what our country has undergone. These four last months have seemed to me age-long. By thousands have our brave ones been mown down; wives, mothers, are weeping for those they shall never see again; hearths are desolate; dire poverty spreads; anguish increases. I have traversed the greater part of the districts most terribly devastated in my diocese; and the ruins I beheld were more dreadful than I, prepared by the saddest of forebodings, could have imagined. Churches, schools, asylums, hospitals, convents, in great numbers, are in ruins. Entire villages have all but disappeared.

In the dear city of Louvain, perpetually in my thoughts, the magnificent church of St. Peter will never recover its former splendor. The ancient college of St. Ives, the art schools, the consular and commercial schools of the University, the old markets, our rich library with its collections, its unique and unpublished manuscripts, its archives, its galleries — all this accumulation of intellectual, of historic, of artistic riches, the fruits of the labor of five centuries — all is in the dust.

Many a parish has lost its pastor. In my diocese alone I know that thirteen priests were put to death. Thousands of Belgian citizens have been deported to the prisons of Germany. Hundreds of innocent men have been shot or burned. We can neither number our dead nor complete the measure of our ruins.

And there where lives were not taken, and there where the stones of buildings were not thrown down, what anguish unrevealed! Families, hitherto living at ease, now in bitter want; all commerce at an end; all careers ruined; industry at a standstill; thousands upon thousands of workingmen without employment; workingwomen, shop girls, humble servant girls, without the means of earning their bread; and poor souls forlorn on the bed of sickness and fever, crying, "O Lord, how long, how long?" There is nothing to reply. The reply is the secret of God.

Yes, dearest brethren, it is the secret of God. He is the master of events and the sovereign director of the human multitude. As for us, my brethren, we will adore Him in the integrity of our souls. Not yet do we see, in all its magnificence, the revelation of His wisdom, but our faith trusts Him with it all. Before His justice we are humble, and in His mercy hopeful.

God will save Belgium, my brethren, you cannot doubt it. Nay, rather He is saving her. Across the smoke of conflagration, across the stream of blood, have you not glimpses, do you not perceive, signs of His love for us? Is there a patriot among us who does not know that Belgium has grown great? Nay, which of us would have the heart to cancel this last page in the national history? Which of us does not exult in the brightness of the glory of this shattered nation? When a mighty foreign power, confident in its own strength and defiant of the faith of treaties, dared to threaten us in our independence, then did all Belgians rise as one man.

Belgium gave her word of honor to defend her independence. She kept her word. The other Powers had agreed to protect and to respect Belgian neutrality. Germany has broken her word; England has been faithful to it. These are the facts. We should have acted unworthily had we evaded our obligation. And now we would not rescind our first resolution; we exult in it. Being called upon to write a most solemn page in the history of our country, we resolved that it should be also a sincere, also a glorious page. And as long as we are compelled to give proof of endurance, so long we shall endure.

Truce then, my brethren, to all murmurs of complaint. Not only to the Redeemer's example shall you look but also to the example of the thirty thousand, perhaps forty thousand, men who have already shed their life blood for their country. In comparison with them what have you endured who are deprived of the daily comforts of your lives? Let the patriotism of our army, the heroism of our King and of our beloved Queen, serve to stimulate us and support us. Let us bemoan ourselves no more. Let us deserve the coming deliverance. Let us hasten it by our prayers. Courage, brethren. Suffering passes away; the crown of life for our souls, the crown of glory for our nation, shall not pass.

TO BELGIUM
EDEN PHILLPOTTS

Champion of human honour, let us lave
  Your feet and bind your wounds on bended knee.
  Though coward hands have nailed you to the tree
And shed your innocent blood and dug your grave,

Rejoice and live! Your oriflamme shall wave
  While man has power to perish and be free —
  A golden flame of holiest Liberty,
Proud as the dawn and as the sunset brave.

Belgium, where dwelleth reverence for right
  Enthroned above all ideals; where your fate
And your supernal patience and your might
  Most sacred grow in human estimate,
You shine a star above this stormy night,
  Little no more, but infinitely great.

LIEGE

WILLIAM WATSON

Betwixt the foe and France was she,
  France the immortal, France the Free;
The foe like one vast living sea
  Drew nigh.

He dreamed that none his tide would stay
  But when he bade her to make way,
She, through her cannon, answered, "Nay
  Not I."

No tremor and no fear she showed;
  She held the pass, she barred the road
While Death's unsleeping feet bestrode
  The ground.

So long as deeds of noblest worth
  Are sung 'mid joy and tears and mirth,
Her glory shall to the ends of earth
  Resound.

Watched by a world that yearned to aid,
   Lonely she stood but undismayed,
Resplendent was the part she played,
   And pure.

Praised be her heroes, proud her sons;
   She threw her souls into the guns.
Her name shall with the loveliest ones
   Endure.

LA BRABANÇONNE
FLORENCE ATTENBOROUGH

The years of slavery are past,
The Belgian rejoices once more;
Courage restores to him at last
The rights he held of yore!

Strong and firm his clasp will be,
Keeping the ancient flag unfurl'd
To fling its message on the watchful world:
For King, for Right, and Liberty!

For thee, dear country, cherished motherland,
Our songs and our valour we give;
Never from thee our hearts are banned,
For thee alone we live!

And thy years shall glorious be,
Circled in Unity's embrace,
Thy sons shall cherish thee in ev'ry place
For King, for Right, and Liberty.

THE FIGHTERS OF FRANCE[1]
ANATOLE FRANCE

Dear soldiers, dear fellow-citizens, I address you because I love you and honor you and think of you unceasingly.

I am entitled to speak to you heart to heart because I have a right to speak for France, being one of those who have ever sought, in freedom of judgment and uprightness of conscience, the best means of making their country strong. I am entitled to speak to you because not having desired war, but being compelled to suffer it, I, like you, like all Frenchmen, am resolved to wage it till the end, until justice shall have conquered iniquity, civilization barbarism, and until the nations are delivered from the monstrous menace of an oppressive militarism. I have a right to speak to you because I am one of the few who have never deceived you, and who have never believed that you needed lies for the maintenance of your courage; one of the few who, rejecting as unworthy of you deceptive fictions and misleading silence, have told you the truth.

I told you in December last year: This war will be cruel and long. I tell you now: You have done much, but all is not yet over. The end of your labors approaches, but is not yet. You are fighting against an enemy fortified by long preparation and immense material. Your foe is unscrupulous. He has learned from his leaders that inhumanity is the soldier's first virtue. Arming himself in a manner undreamed of hitherto by the most

---
[1] Extract from an article in *Petit Parisien* in 1915; translated by Winifred Stevens, editor of "The Book of France."

M. ANATOLE FRANCE

formidable of conquerors, he causes rivers of blood to flow and breathes forth vapors charged with torpor and with death. Endure, persevere, dare. Remain what you are, and none shall prevail against you.

You are fighting for your native land, that laughing, fertile land, the most beautiful in the world; for your fields and your meadows. For the august mother, who, crowned with vine leaves and with ears of corn, waits to welcome you and to feed you with all the inexhaustible treasures of her breast. You are fighting for your village belfry, your roofs of slate or tile, with wreaths of smoke curling up into the serene sky. For your fathers' graves, your children's cradles.

You are fighting for our august cities, on the banks of whose rivers rise the monuments of generations — romanesque churches, cathedrals, minsters, abbeys, palaces, triumphal arches, columns of bronze, theaters, museums, town halls, hospitals, statues of sages and of heroes — monuments whose walls, whether modest or magnificent, shelter alike commerce, industry, science, and the arts, all that constitutes the beauty of life.

You are fighting for our moral heritage, our manners, our uses, our laws, our customs, our beliefs, our traditions. For the works of our sculptors, our architects, our painters, our engravers, our goldsmiths, our enamelers, our glass cutters, our weavers. For the songs of our musicians. For our mother tongue which, with ineffable sweetness, for eight centuries has flowed from the lips of our poets, our orators, our historians, our philosophers. For the knowledge of man and of nature. For that encyclopedic learning which attained among us the high-water mark of precision and lucidity. You are fighting for the genius of France, which enlightened the world and gave freedom to the nations. By this noble spirit bastiles are overthrown. And, lastly, you are fighting for the homes of Belgians, English, Russians, Italians, Serbians, not for France merely, but for Europe, ceaselessly disturbed and furiously threatened by Germany's devouring ambition.

The Fatherland! Liberty! Beloved children of France, these are the sacred treasures committed to your keeping; for their sakes you endure; for their sakes you will conquer.

THE MARSEILLAISE
ROUGET DE LISLE

Ye sons of freedom, wake to glory!
   Hark! Hark! what myriads bid you rise!
Your children, wives, and grandsires hoary,
   Behold their tears and hear their cries!
Shall hateful tyrants, mischiefs breeding,
   With hireling hosts, a ruffian band,
   Affright and desolate the land,
While peace and liberty lie bleeding?
   To arms! to arms, ye brave!
   The avenging sword unsheathe!
March on! march on! all hearts resolved
   On victory or death!

Now, now the dangerous storm is rolling,
   Which treacherous kings, confederate, raise;
The dogs of war, let loose, are howling,
   And lo! our fields and cities blaze;
And shall we basely view the ruin,
   While lawless force, with guilty stride,

  Spreads desolation far and wide,
With crimes and blood his hands imbruing!
  To arms! to arms, ye brave!
  The avenging sword unsheathe!
March on! march on! all hearts resolved
  On victory or death!

With luxury and pride surrounded,
  The vile, insatiate despots dare,
Their thirst of power and gold unbounded,
  To meet and vend the light and air;
Like beasts of burden would they load us,
  Like gods would bid their slaves adore;
  But man is man, and who is more?
Then, shall they longer lash and goad us?
  To arms! to arms, ye brave!
  The avenging sword unsheathe!
March on! march on! all hearts resolved
  On victory or death!

YOUR LAD, AND MY LAD
RANDALL PARRISH

Down toward the deep-blue water, marching to throb of drum,
From city street and country lane the lines of khaki come;
The rumbling guns, the sturdy tread, are full of grim appeal,
While rays of western sunshine flash back from burnished steel.
With eager eyes and cheeks aflame the serried ranks advance;
And your dear lad, and my dear lad, are on their way to France.

A sob clings choking in the throat, as file on file sweep by,
Between those cheering multitudes, to where the great ships lie;
The batteries halt, the columns wheel, to clear-toned bugle-call,
With shoulders squared and faces front they stand a khaki wall.
Tears shine on every watcher's cheek, love speaks in every glance;
For your dear lad, and my dear lad, are on their way to France.

Before them, through a mist of years, in soldier buff or blue,
Brave comrades from a thousand fields watch now in proud review;
The same old Flag, the same old Faith — the Freedom of the World —
Spells Duty in those flapping folds above long ranks unfurled.
Strong are the hearts which bear along Democracy's advance,
As your dear lad, and my dear lad, go on their way to France.

The word rings out; a million feet tramp forward on the road,
Along that path of sacrifice o'er which their fathers strode.
With eager eyes and cheeks aflame, with cheers on smiling lips,
These fighting men of '17 move onward to their ships.
Nor even love may hold them back, or halt that stern advance,
As your dear lad, and my dear lad, go on their way to France.

LILLE, LAON, AND ST. DIÉ
JOHN FINLEY

I

Lille, Laon, and St. Dié!
What memories, from far away,
When happy France was wont to be
Weaving her peaceful tapestry
And singing by her clacking loom
Amid her gardens all a-bloom —
What memories, from far away,
Of France's joyous yesterday
Rise through the dimming mists of years,
The smoke of battle and the tears
Of those who daily look across
The furrowed, crimsoned fields of loss
Ploughed all the trenched and barbéd way
From Lille to Laon and St. Dié.

II

Lille!
Long, long ago I was in Lille; —
E'en then a veil did half conceal
Her face, but not the fleecy rack
Of clouds upon the shrieking track
Of shell and shrapnel bearing death;
It was the sweet sea-vapor's breath
Encircling her as if in fear
I'd see the living Tête de Cire
And ne'er contented be elsewhere
In this then peaceful world. 'Twas there
They made for me a regal feast;
But now we here who have the least

Have more than they who had the most
And played so gallantly the host; —
And so, as my own prayer is said:
"Give us this day our daily bread,"
For those who hunger, too, I pray
In Lille and Laon and St. Dié.

III

Laon!
I climbed to Laon above the plain
Where now the Teuton battle-stain
Colors the crag, to find the spot
Where he was born who left his lot
Of luxury to bear Christ's name
To savages that fought with dart
And tomahawk, but knew no art
To match the red atrocity
That now holds Laon, in blasphemy
Of that same Father of us all.
Would Père Marquette would come and call
These heathen to repentance ere
The *Strafe* and *Krieg* and answ'ring *guerre*
Shall make the whole wide world a hell!—
But if he cannot, we who dwell
In this free land whose mightiest flood
He found, will give our mingled blood
To wash that brutish stain away
From Lille and Laon and St. Dié.

IV

And St. Dié!
Dear is this village of the Vosges
List'ning afar the Marne's *éloge*

And to herself repeating o'er
The word she whisp'ring spoke before
All others in the world — a word
That all the planet since has heard —
"America!" Here was the spring
Of our loved country's christening;
Here in this cloistered scholar's haunt
Was our New World baptismal font,
Now scarred and blackened by the guns
Of Europe's scientific Huns.
America, from that same bowl
Thou'lt be baptized anew in soul;
But not by water, by the fire
Of thine own sacrosanct desire
For right, flashing in carmine spray
From Lille to Laon and St. Dié.

V

Lille, Laon, and St. Dié!
Our battle front, as theirs to-day
Who fight for France, all unafraid
Of death, weary but undismayed,
To help push back the green-gray line
That it may never leave the Rhine
Again to menace all the good
Of long-dreamed human brotherhood.
Here shall our France-befriended land
Take now its sacrificial stand;
Fight for a free humanity,
Fight for the thing that ought to be,
And our great debt to France repay
At Lille and Laon and St. Dié.

VIVIANI AT SPRINGFIELD[1]

Gentlemen and Ladies:

Before coming here we went to the field of silence to lay quick-fading flowers on the immortal tomb of Abraham Lincoln and bear to his shade the greeting of all France.

And I would have you know that however great the distance between Springfield and France may be, the radiance of his noble face has long been known in our native land. In no democracy did any man offer the world a purer image than he by his noble career. That career is far better known by you than by me. You know that, born of the people, the son of a man who could not read, after having in his youth suffered every sort of privation, he rose through silent meditation, by study, to the full cultivation of his mind and the full development of his will. You know that silently he rose to the summit of civic honor; and that from the summit he had attained he looked with untroubled gaze upon a great, an heroic, a tragic duty; he knew that the minds of men cannot without abasement live in contact with injustice. And that is why whatever pity and compassion rent his soul, since the equality of all human beings must needs be proclaimed, since the laws must needs rise to the level of man's dignity in all places, he let loose civil war upon his native land—that civil war whose heroes we have seen in their old age reconciled, wherever we have passed. On the morrow of his gigantic enterprise he died. He cannot be said to have been buried in his triumph; that triumph will last as long as an American is left to revere it, and

---
[1] Delivered May 7, 1917.

RENÉ RAPHAEL VIVIANI

we have come here to salute his great memory in the name of France, of the French Republic. But permit me to recall with just pride that the French of the French Revolution, of the Revolution of 1848, also proclaimed the rights of man. And this shows that all democracies, in spite of distance and time, are one. And when three years ago Imperial Germany in arms, without provocation, without a shadow of excuse, by right of force alone, rushed on France, tore up international rights and violated all human consciences, France with her allies defended those eternal principles. For three years she has defended them. And now America in turn, rises to their defense at the call of her illustrious President, Mr. Wilson, who, too, though a man of thought and a philosopher, has seen he must become a man of action when these eternal principles exacted reparation and vengeance.

Now we are all united in this great struggle, to defend right and justice. We feel as if at every step in this blissful valley we have found old memories of our beloved motherland, as if we had never left it. Here we find the shades and memories of our forefathers. But is it enough to evoke these memories in a speech? Must we bury all our ardent hopes in our hearts? I shall not forget, but transmit to my fellow countrymen your desire to pay back your debt of gratitude to France, in memory of Lafayette who brought here help and French soldiers to fight for American independence. But permit me, without any thought of diminishing the effect of your words, to define their full sense. It is not to France your debt lies. What France did for America, she did for liberty, with no thought of exacting a reward for it some day. It is to all humanity your debt of gratitude should be paid:

humanity and France here are one. Yes, it is because that noble land has at all times in its history held in its hands the fate of the world: it is because on our territory which seems to have been chosen by history as the meeting place for all combats and immolations, the fate of the world has so often been decided; because our children with their hearts, their arms, their hands, their brains, are struggling even now to keep liberty from perishing, to keep disaster away from the whole world; it is because of all that you have risen in arms. And when you rally to France, you rally to the cause of liberty, of right, of democracy.

Come, then. We will bear away from your land the memory of these meetings of free citizens, and, when we return to our country, when the free citizens of republican France ask us what we have seen, we will answer: We have seen crowds tumultuous in their joy, enthusiastic crowds, but they came not forth to see alone, to gaze on passing men: they came as to some great duty, to acclaim France through us. We will take back the words of all your orators; we will tell what you think, what you desire, what you hope for from the future, not only a free and delivered France, but a regenerate Europe.

And when this great work shall have been accomplished, American brothers, faithful to the traditions of Washington and Abraham Lincoln, you may return in pious pilgrimage to Mount Vernon and to the graveyard of Springfield and there bow in silent reverence before the two pure heroes of your race. You will most surely have served their memory; and rest assured that by so doing you will have broadened yet the glorious annals of the American Republic.

THE FATHERLAND
JAMES RUSSELL LOWELL

Where is the true man's fatherland?
    Is it where he by chance is born?
    Doth not the yearning spirit scorn
In such scant borders to be spanned?
Oh! yes! his fatherland must be
As the blue heaven wide and free!

Where'er a human heart doth wear
    Job's myrtle-wreath or sorrow's gyves,
    Where'er a human spirit strives
After a life more true and fair,
There is the true man's birthplace grand,
His is a world-wide fatherland!

THE BLUE AND THE GRAY IN FRANCE
GEORGE MORROW MAYO

Here's to the Blue of the wind-swept North,
    When we meet on the fields of France;
May the spirit of Grant be with you all
    As the sons of the North advance.

And here's to the Gray of the sun-kissed South,
    When we meet on the fields of France;
May the spirit of Lee be with you all
    As the sons of the South advance.

And here's to the Blue and the Gray as one,
    When we meet on the fields of France;
May the spirit of God be with us all
    As the sons of the Flag advance.

A WELCOME TO MARSHAL JOFFRE[1]
CHARLES SEYMOUR WHITMAN

It is singularly fitting that New York State should first bid welcome to our visitors from the French Republic, at Washington's military home in Newburgh. This place, peculiarly precious to Americans, is not without French associations and memories. Here, giving aid and comfort, counsel and support, to the leader of our armies, lived for many weeks the great son of France, Lafayette, and as we recall the events of those dark days of struggle and of privation, we realize that Americans and Frenchmen have been allies before.

Those from whom you drew your being came to our fathers then, fighting as they were for human rights, for justice and for liberty. Aided by France, after seven years of struggle, the cause was won, and a nation destined to be mighty was brought forth upon this continent.

Three peoples were represented in the Revolutionary War — English, French, Americans. Armies sent by a stupid and stubborn monarch did not prevail against the spirit and the character of a people who themselves drew their inspiration and their strength from their ancestors over the sea and who in themselves embodied and represented that which was greatest and best in England's history and England's tradition far more truly than did the English king who sent his soldiers here.

Again, the representatives of these three peoples meet on American soil. Again, the French and the Americans

[1] Delivered May 11, 1917, at the Washington headquarters at Newburgh, New York.

Charles S. Whitman

CHARLES C. WHITMAN

are found in Washington's headquarters. Again a stubborn and arrogant ruler has plunged his nation into war. Despotism gone mad has filled the world with terror. But the Frenchman and the Englishman and the American are not divided now. The nation whose existence was made possible by our French ally over a century ago — composed to-day as it is of people from all lands, speaking many languages, with natural affections, some of them, for ancestral homes over the sea — is united in devotion and loyalty to the flag and all for which it stands. We realize that our allies in Europe are fighting for civilization, as truly as did our fathers fight here; that the struggle is a struggle for humanity to-day, as truly as it was in 1776, and that no price is too high to pay, no sacrifice too great to make, for the holy cause for which the sons of Great Britain and France are offering their all.

We are with these people, battling for the right. Their cause is our cause. We have engaged our lives, our liberty and our sacred honor that a shadow may be lifted from the world and that humanity may be rescued from an evil and abominable thing.

Peace will come again — a peace purchased with the blood of martyrs. If the sacrifice is to be worth while — if those dead shall not have died in vain, — that peace must come only with absolute, complete and final victory.

On behalf of the State, which is willing and more than willing, prepared and ready, to do all that she may be called upon to do in your cause and in ours, I bid you welcome. The name of the hero of the Marne is as truly a household word in the land which Lafayette came to save as it is in the land which gave him birth.

"Welcome" is an easy word to say, and I realize that

to those whose lives have been what yours have been during the last months and years, words may seem like empty things. It is a privilege, however, for us to express the admiration, the affection and the reverence that our people have grown to possess for the men and for the women of France. It is perhaps impossible for us to realize all that you have been called upon to endure or to appreciate all that you have suffered as you have made for your country a place in the hearts and affections of mankind which no other nation has ever held.

I know that I express the honest sentiment of the people of the State of New York: "God save, and God bless, the Republic of France!"

THE NIGHTINGALES OF FLANDERS
GRACE HAZARD CONKLING

The nightingales of Flanders,
  They have not gone to war.
A soldier heard them singing
  Where they had sung before.

The earth was torn and quaking,
  The sky about to fall;
The nightingales of Flanders,
  They minded not at all.

At intervals he heard them
  Between the guns, he said,
Making a thrilling music
  Above the listening dead.

Of woodland and of orchard
  And roadside tree bereft,
The nightingales of Flanders
  Were singing *"France is left!"*

SOMEWHERE IN FRANCE

HARVEY M. WATTS

"Somewhere in France" they'll bivouac 'neath the sky,
As poplared roads lead straightway to the front
Where the scarred towns have borne the frightful brunt
Of gun and mine; and all things open lie,
A cratered desert, grim, where none may ply
  The trades of Peace; but, used to death, full blunt,
  From trench to trench the hidden foe must hunt,
Giving no quarter as they sullen fly!
"Somewhere in France"—This is the only hope
  To save from those who batten on the slain,
  To meet the menace of this armored might—
Where Joan was victor they must more than cope,
  Or else the rumbling tocsin sounds in vain,
  And all that man achieved sinks into night!

THE CHILDREN OF FRANCE
MARSHAL JOFFRE

Among all the innumerable expressions of sympathy, all the kindnesses showered by you on France, none touches us so deeply as what you are doing for the orphans of our heroic dead. Our children are our most precious possession, our joy and our hope, and there is no surer way to our hearts than to help these little ones, the most pitiful victims of this war for the liberation of the world. In their name, in the name of our soldiers of France, I thank you, I thank the children of America whose hearts have gone out to their stricken little French brothers and sisters. The memory of what you have done, of what you are doing, will never fade. You have sown the seeds of love and friendship between our two countries. They will flower when they are men and women. Between America and France there is now a tender bond of human kindness and affection that nothing can break.

THE VICTOR OF THE MARNE
ROBERT UNDERWOOD JOHNSON

Adown the bright and fluttering street
    Let serried thousands throng,
And children march with eager feet
    In phalanxes of song,
That Memory to their latest
    Heirs his glorious deed prolong.

Copyright by Mayor's Reception Committee N.Y
MARSHALL JOFFRE

GRAND-PÈRE
ROBERT W. SERVICE

And so when he reached my bed
The General made a stand:
"My brave young fellow," he said,
 "I would shake your hand."

So I lifted my arm, the right,
With never a hand at all:
Only a stump, a sight
 Fit to appal.

"Well, well. Now that's too bad!
That's sorrowful luck," he said;
"But there! You give me, my lad,
 The left instead."

So from under the blanket's rim
I raised and showed him the other,
A snag as ugly and grim
 As its ugly brother.

He looked at each jagged wrist;
He looked, but he did not speak;
And then he bent down and kissed
 Me on either cheek.

You wonder now I don't mind
I hadn't a hand to offer . . .
They tell me (you know I'm blind)
 'Twas Grand-père Joffre.

CHILDREN OF FRANCE
GERTRUDE ROBINSON

Dear little sad-eyed children of France,
Once on a time, when the world was gay,
In the streets of Paris you danced and sang,
  God grant you again a happy day,
    Sad little children of France.

Wan little weary-eyed children of France,
  In the streets of Paris you knelt today,
Knelt at the sight of a succoring flag,
  Knelt in the streets where you used to play,
    Heartbroken children of France.

We are thinking today of the long ago,
  Kneeling children beyond the sea,
When your fathers came, with hearts aflame,
  To us, in the name of liberty,
    Fatherless children of France.

Fair by the side of the Red, White and Blue
  The Stars and Stripes in your streets are a-blow
Never so beautiful, now they glow
  In the name of that help of the long ago,
    Kneeling babies of France.

You knelt in your streets as our flag went by —
  Our flag with a glory strangely new.
The stars of heaven gleamed in its folds,
  Strewn but today in that field of blue,
    For you, O children of France!

CHILDREN OF FRANCE

Dear little war-smitten children of France,
  In our hearts is a prayer as the flag goes by —
For the flag we have vowed to a glorious quest,
  For the flag aflame on a far away sky,
    For God — and the babies of France.

FRATERNAL MESSAGE TO AMERICA[1]
GABRIELE D'ANNUNZIO

For the soul of Italy to-day the Capitol at Washington has become a beacon-light. Now the group of stars on the banner of the great Republic has become a constellation of the spring, like the Pleiades; a propitious sign to sailors, armed and unarmed alike; a spiritual token for all nations fighting a righteous war. I give the salute of Italy, of the Roman Capitol to the Capitol at Washington; a salute to the people of the Union, who now confirm and seal the pledge that liberty shall be preserved. The spontaneous act consummated by the people of George Washington is a glorious sacrifice on behalf of the hopes of all mankind.

Our war is not destructive. It is creative. With all manner of atrocities, all manner of shameful acts, the barbarian has striven to destroy the idea which, until this struggle began, man had of man. The barbarian multiplied on the innocent, infamous outrages inspired by hate, alternating senile impudence and brutal stupidity. The barbarian ground heroism to earth, cast down the airy cathedrals where congregated the aspirations of the eternal soul, burned the seats of wisdom decked with the flowers of all the arts; distorted the lineaments of Christ, tore off the garments of the Virgin.

Now once again we begin to have hope of the nobility of man. Love's face is radiant, though its eyes are moist with tears, for never was love so much beloved. Love overflows on all the world like a brook in May.

---
[1] Sent April 7, 1917, on our entrance into war.

Copyright by Underwood & Underwood

GABRIELE D'ANNUNZIO

GABRIELE D'ANNUNZIO

Our hearts are not large enough to gather it and to hold it. The people of Lincoln, springing to their feet to defend the eternal spirit of man to-day, increase immeasurably this sum of love opposed to fury, the fury of the barbarian.

ON THE ITALIAN FRONT, MCMXVI
GEORGE EDWARD WOODBERRY

"I will die cheering, if I needs must die;
  So shall my last breath write upon my lips
    Viva Italia! when my spirit slips
Down the great darkness from the mountain sky;
And those who shall behold me where I lie
  Shall murmur: 'Look, you! how his spirit dips
    From glory into glory! the eclipse
Of death is vanquished! Lo, his victor-cry!'

"Live, thou, upon my lips, Italia mine,
  The sacred death-cry of my frozen clay!
Let thy dear light from my dead body shine
  And to the passer-by thy message say:
'*Ecco!* though heaven has made my skies divine,
  My sons' love sanctifies my soil for aye!'"

DECLARATION OF WAR BY ITALY
GABRIELE D'ANNUNZIO

Now the arm of Rome was raised, the right hand of Rome was lifted to shake and to shatter,
But we beheld our signs no more: there was no prophet among us, nor any that knew how long . . .
The bombs rumble over Monte Nero: the guns thunder over Piedmont . . .

The dead, O, Italy: thy dead . . .
Then was heard from on high a voice without flesh which said,
"Blessed are the dead!": a voice made itself felt, announcing, "Blessed are those that die for thee!" . . .
The dead shall have a new song: and the desert shall be sanctified.

OUT OF ROME

CLINTON SCOLLARD

Out of Rome they march as when
Scipio led his serried men,
  While the cry of "Viva!   Viva!"
Rings again and yet again.

They, in dreams of high desire,
Rousing them to holy ire,
  On the Capitolian altars
Have beheld the vestal fire.

Rear and vanguard, first and last,
They have caught the virile, vast,
  Emulous centurion ardour
From some legion of the past.

Win they laurel wreath or rue,
We must feel that this is true,
  That the ancient Roman valour
Thrills through Italy anew!

TO THE YOUNG MEN OF ITALY
GIUSEPPE MAZZINI

The Italian movement, my countrymen, is, by decree of Providence, that of Europe. We arise to give a pledge of moral progress to the European world. But neither political fictions, nor dynastic aggrandizements, nor theories of expediency, can transform or renovate the life of the peoples. Humanity lives and moves through faith; great principles are the guiding stars that lead Europe toward the future. Let us turn to the graves of our martyrs, and ask inspiration of those who died for us all, and we shall find the secret of victory in the adoration of a faith. The angel of martyrdom and the angel of victory are brothers; but the one looks up to heaven, and the other looks down to earth; and it is when, from epoch to epoch, their glance meets between earth and heaven, that creation is embellished with a new life and a people arises from the cradle or the tomb, evangelist or prophet. . . .

Love your country. Your country is the land where your parents sleep, where is spoken that language in which the chosen of your heart, blushing, whispered the first word of love; it is the home that God has given you, that, by striving to perfect yourselves therein, you may prepare to ascend to Him. It is your name, your glory, your sign among the people. Give to it your thoughts, your counsels, your blood. Raise it up, great and beautiful as it was foretold by our great men, and see that you leave it uncontaminated by any trace of falsehood or of servitude; unprofaned by dismemberment. Let it be one, as the thought of God. You are twenty-five millions of men, endowed with active, splendid faculties; possessing a tradition of glory the envy of the nations of Europe. An immense future is before you; you lift your eyes to the loveliest heaven, and around you smiles the loveliest land in Europe; you are encircled by the Alps and the sea, boundaries traced out by the finger of God for a people of giants — you are bound to be such, or to be nothing. . . .

Love humanity. You can only ascertain your own mission from the aim set by God before humanity at large. God has given you your country as cradle and humanity as mother; you can not rightly love your brethren of the cradle if you love not the common mother. Beyond the Alps, beyond the sea, are other peoples now fighting or preparing to fight the holy fight of independence, of nationality, of liberty; other peoples striving by different routes to reach the same goal — improvement, association, and the foundation of an authority which shall put an end to moral anarchy and relink the earth to heaven; an authority which mankind may love and obey without remorse or shame. Unite with them; they will unite with you. Do not invoke their aid where your single arm can suffice to conquer; but say to them that the hour will shortly sound for a terrible struggle between right and blind force, and that in that hour you will ever be found with those who have raised the same banner as yourselves.

And love, young men, love and venerate the ideal. The ideal is the Word of God. High above every country, high above humanity, is the country of the spirit, the city of the soul, in which all are brethren who believe in the inviolability of thought and in the dignity of our immortal soul; and the baptism of this fraternity is martyrdom.

From that high sphere spring the principles which alone can redeem the peoples. Arise for the sake of these, and not from impatience of suffering or dread of evil. Anger, pride, ambition, and the desire of material prosperity are arms common alike to the peoples and their oppressors, and even should you conquer with these to-day, you would fall again to-morrow; but principles belong to the peoples alone, and their oppressors can find no arms to oppose them. Adore enthusiasm, the dreams of the virgin soul and the visions of early youth, for they are a perfume of paradise which the soul retains in issuing from the hands of its Creator. Respect above all things your conscience; have upon your lips the truth implanted by God in your hearts, and while laboring in harmony, even with those who differ from you, in all that tends to the emancipation of our soil, yet ever bear your own banner erect and boldly promulgate your own faith. . . .

God be with you, and bless Italy!

SERBIA'S SACRIFICE[1]
MAJOR STOBART

As Serbian politicians looked from the heights of their Serbian mountains upon the glories of their fertile land, a land of corn and bread, a land of wine and vineyards, they must have heard the Tempter's words, whispering as of old, "All these things will I give you if — if — you will fall down and worship militarism and the Central Powers." But with one voice the Serbian people answered, "Get thee behind me, Satan. It is written in our hearts, 'Thou shalt worship Freedom: her only shalt thou serve.'" Thus Serbia, the latest evoked of the European nations, perceived with an insight at which history will one day marvel, the inner, the true interpretation of the word "nation." She perceived that the life force of a nation is a spiritual force, and is not dependent on material conditions for existence. Serbia had existed during five hundred years of material annihilation under Turkish rule. Through all that wilderness of time the ideal of freedom had been her pillar of cloud by day and of fire by night, pointing to the Promised Land. Serbia is again in the wilderness, and the same light guides and cheers her. She is full of courageous faith, because she understands that a nation means, primarily, not physical country (mountains, rivers, valleys), not State, not Government, but a free and united spirit. That is the only definition which allows of the indefinite expansion which will some day include all human kind in one united nation. Serbia is full of faith and hope,

---
[1] From *The Flaming Sword in Serbia and Elsewhere.*

Major St. Clair Stobart

because she knows that she is not, and never will be, deprived of nationhood.

In some minor ways Serbia may, in her civilization, have been behind other nations in the west of Europe, but she was ahead of Western Europe in that one thing which is of real importance, that one thing which cannot be copied or learned from other nations, and which is therefore either innate or unachievable: Serbia is ahead of other nations in her power of sacrificing herself for ideals. All nations are ready to sacrifice life for nationhood. Serbia made first this common sacrifice, but when that did not avail, she voluntarily, for the sake of an abstract and spiritual ideal, made the supreme sacrifice, the sacrifice of country, the sacrifice for which other nations make the penultimate sacrifice of life. The Serbian people sacrificed their country rather than bow the knee to militarism and foreign tyranny; they sacrificed their country in Utopian quest for the right, both for themselves and for other Slav brethren, to work out their own salvation in spiritual freedom. A people with such ideals, and with such power of sacrifice, must be worthy of a great future.

SERBIA
AMELIA JOSEPHINE BURR

Hark, from the East a keen and bitter cry —
  New tears are flowing in the furrows of old sorrow.
On your wasted fields your dead drift like fallen leaves;
  Only the Pale Harvester garners heavy sheaves.
How have you the courage to struggle toward tomorrow,
Serbia, Serbia, land that will not die?

I have stood for freedom—freedom can not perish.
I have stood for honor—honor must endure.
But my children starve, the children who should cherish
For the world's to-morrow my spirit flaming-pure.
You who sit in safety, you whose babes are fed,
You who by the peril of other men are free,
Listen to my living, ere the hour be sped,
Lest you hear forever the silence of my dead.
Serbia, Serbia, God hears. Do we?

SCARRED

Far nobler the sword that is nicked and worn,
Far fairer the flag that is grimy and torn,
Than when to the battle fresh they were borne.

He was tried and found true; He stood the test;
'Neath whirlwinds of doubt, when all the rest
Crouched down and submitted, He fought best.

There are wounds on His breast that can never be healed
There are gashes that bleed and may not be sealed,
But, wounded and gashed, He won the field.

And others may dream in their easy chairs,
And point their white hands to the scars He bears;
And the palm and the laurel are His—not theirs.

SALONIKA IN NOVEMBER
BRIAN HILL

Up above the gray hills the wheeling birds are calling
  Round about the cold gray hills in never-resting flight
Far along the marshes a drifting mist is falling,
  Scattered tents and sandy plain melt into the night

SALONIKA IN NOVEMBER

Round about the gray hills rumbles distant thunder,
  Echoes of the mighty guns firing night and day,—
Gray guns, long guns, that smite the hills asunder,
  Grumbling and rumbling, and telling of the fray.

Out among the islands twinkling lights are glowing,
  Distant little fairy lights, that gleam upon the bay;
All along the broken road gray transport wagons going
  Up to where the long gray guns roar and crash alway.

Up above the cold gray hills the wheel-birds are crying,
  Brother calls to brother, as they pass in restless flight.
Lost souls, dead souls, voices of the dying,
  Circle o'er the hills of Greece and wail into the night.

—From *The Poetry Review*

WOMAN'S DUTY[1]
MRS. PERCY V. PENNYBACKER

There was never greater need for women to be sane than at this hour. There is no excuse for excitement or for hysteria. If our men are to give the best that is in them, we must keep the atmosphere of our homes sweet and serene. Remember, no sacrifice is a great sacrifice unless it is made *cheerfully*. Let there be no weeping, no complaining, no lamentation, when our beloved ones answer the call to duty.

This is also a time for moral sanity and for lofty ideals. I wish I could burn into the heart of every young woman the remark that a distinguished military man made a few days ago: "The influence of young women on soldiers is terrifying in its strength; it is not what a woman says, it is not what a woman does, it is what she really *is* that counts. Men sense inmost beliefs. Men raise or lower their ideals as she dictates." This is an awful responsibility, young women, but it is yours; you cannot escape it. In these days of distress, every woman should pass her soul in review before herself and ask: "What are my standards? Do I really believe that the Commandments were given for men as well as for women? Do I realize that I am in part 'my brother's keeper'?" In dress, in speech, in manner, in thought, are the young women of America doing their full duty to help our boys in the ranks to retain the loftiest ideals of womanhood, to live clean lives, to take as much pride in moral as in physical victory? It is the duty of every woman in this

[1] From a speech delivered July 6, 1917.

country to help, because the happiness of all is at stake!—the salvation of the next generation is in peril.

It is the duty of women—the special duty—to see that no hate enters into our hearts. If we banish this monster, our husbands, sons and lovers will find it easier to shut their souls to hate. President Wilson has well said, "We are not making war on the German people." This is a holy war, and in such a struggle there is no place for hatred. No one who has lived in Germany, as some of us have, and has known the lovely home life, can hate the German people. No one who has been ill in Germany, as some of us have, and has received generous kindness and consideration, can hate the German people. No one who has studied history aright and has learned the contributions made to the happiness of the world by the men and women of Germany, can hate the German people.

As I sit in church on Sunday and see the Cross borne down the aisle, my heart is thrilled when I behold that now, side by side with the Cross, comes the Flag. At the altar they stand like twin sentinels guarding the Holy of Holies. I love to think of our America today as a gracious, beautiful matron. In her hour of peril, before the altar she calls her stalwart sons, she calls her fair young daughters, and says: "My children, behold this Flag, 'the Stars and Stripes'; it has been baptized in blood and sacrifice; it stands for liberty and love; it has never stood for oppression, for tyranny, for conquest. You were born beneath it; it has cherished you; I give it now into your hands. Guard it, die for it, but forget not that with this Flag I give you another—the Flag of Christ—the Flag that has said for two thousand years, and says today, 'Love thy neighbor as thyself.'"

THE BRAVE AT HOME
THOMAS BUCHANAN READ

I

The maid who binds her warrior's sash
  With smile that well her pain dissembles
The while beneath her drooping lash
  One starry tear-drop hangs and trembles
Though Heaven alone records the tear,
  And Fame shall never know her story,
Her heart has shed a drop as dear
  As e're bedewed the field of glory!

II

The wife who girds her husband's sword,
  Mid little ones who weep or wonder,
And bravely speaks the cheering word,
  What though her heart be rent asunder,
Doomed nightly in her dreams to hear
  The bolts of death around him rattle,
Hath shed as sacred blood as e're
  Was poured upon the field of battle!

III

The mother who conceals her grief
  While to her breast her son she presses,
Then breathes a few brave words and brief,
  Kissing the patriot brow she blesses,
With no one but her secret God
  To know the pain that weighs upon her,
Sheds holy blood as e're the sod
  Received on Freedom's field of honor!

TO WOMAN

LAWRENCE BINYON

Your hearts are lifted up, your hearts
That have foreknown the utter price,
Your hearts burn upward like a flame
Of splendor and of sacrifice.

For you too to battle go,
Not with the marching drums and cheers,
But in the watch of solitude
And through the boundless night of fears.

And not a shot comes blind with death
And not a stab of steel is pressed
Home, but invisibly it tore
And entered first a woman's breast.

MOTHERING

LIEUTENANT H. BUCHANAN RYLEY

"He who goes a-mothering finds violets in the lane."—*Old Proverb*.

"Oh, whirl of leaves, Oh, sobbing breeze,
   About the gates of spring,
When the west wind brings the exiles home
   From weary wandering;
And down the rut-worn way they haste —
   God, but their feet are fain!
And he who goes a-mothering
   Finds violets in the lane.

"Dear Lord, throw open wide Thy doors
  For souls to enter in!
The bitter exile over-past
  The home-time shall begin!
Loved hands and lips draw nigh again
  To welcome and to bless,
And the half-forgotten days renew
  Their springtime loveliness.

"Oh, the violets round the Tree of Life,
  Sweet violets round the brim
Of ever-welling water-floods
  Where day grows never dim;

Where tears are dried, and dead hopes raised,
  And so for you and me
Our hearts shall go a-mothering
  For all eternity!"

(This poem written by Lieutenant Ryley was recently sent to *The Living Church* as his last production, with the words: "I have lost two sons in this hellish war and expect to fall myself. But always my heart is in U. S. A., though my duty is on the firing line." He was killed near Jerusalem, December 15, 1917.)

TO A MOTHER
EDEN PHILLPOTTS

Robbed mother of the stricken Motherland—
  Two hearts in one and one among the dead,
  Before your grave with an uncovered head
I, that am man, disquiet and silent stand
In reverence. It is your blood they shed;
  It is your sacred self that they demand,
  For one you bore in joy and hope, and planned
Would make yourself eternal, now has fled.

But though you yielded him unto the knife
    And altar with a royal sacrifice
Of your most precious self and dearer life—
    Your master gem and pearl above all price—
Content you; for the dawn this night restores
Shall be the dayspring of his soul and yours.

ANY WOMAN TO A SOLDIER
GRACE ELLERY CHANNING

The day you march away—let the sun shine,
Let everything be blue and gold and fair,
Triumph of trumpets calling through bright air,
Flags slanting, flowers flaunting—not a sign
That the unbearable is now to bear,
    The day you march away.

The day you march away—this I have sworn,
No matter what comes after, that shall be
Hid secretly between my soul and me
As women hide the unborn—
You shall see brows like banners, lips that frame
Smiles, for the pride those lips have in your name.
You shall see soldiers in my eyes that day—
    That day, my soldier, when you march away.

The day you march away—cannot I guess?
There will be ranks and ranks, all leading on
To one white face, and then—the white face gone,
And nothing left but a gray emptiness—
Blurred moving masses, faceless, featureless—
    The day you march away.

You cannot march away! However far,
Farther and faster still I shall have fled
Before you; and that moment when you land,
Voiceless, invisible, close at your hand
My heart shall smile, hearing the steady tread
      Of your faith-keeping feet.

First at the trenches I shall be to greet;
There's not a watch I shall not share with you;
But more—but most—there where for you the red,
Drenched, dreadful, splendid, sacrificial field lifts up
Inflexible demand,
      I will be there!

My hands shall hold the cup.
My hands beneath your head
Shall bear you—not the stretcher bearer's—through
All anguish of the dying and the dead;
With all your wounds I shall have ached and bled,
Waked, thirsted, starved, been fevered, gasped for breath
Felt the death dew;
And you shall live, because my heart has said
To Death
      That Death itself shall have no part in you

LABOR MUST BEAR ITS PART[1]
WOODROW WILSON

While we are fighting for freedom we must see, among other things, that labor is free, and that means a number of interesting things. It means not only that we must do what we have declared our purpose to do—see that the conditions of labor are not rendered more onerous by the war—but also that we shall see to it that the instrumentalities by which the conditions of labor are improved are not blocked nor checked.

To "stand together" means that nobody must interrupt the processes of our energy if the interruption can possibly be avoided without the absolute invasion of freedom. Nobody has a right to stop the processes of labor until all the methods of conciliation and settlement have been exhausted.

In order to clear the atmosphere and come down to business, everybody on both sides has got to transact business, and the settlement is never impossible when both sides want to do the square and right thing. Moreover, a settlement is always hard to avoid when the parties can be brought face to face. I can differ with a man much more radically when he is n't in the room than I can when he is in the room, because then the awkward thing is that he can come back at me and answer what I say. It is always dangerous for a man to have the floor entirely to himself. And, therefore, we must insist in every instance that the parties come into each other's presence and there discuss the issues between them, and

---

[1] From a speech delivered November 12, 1917.

not separately in places which have no communication with each other.

I like to remind myself of a delightful saying of an Englishman of a past generation, Charles Lamb. He was with a group of friends and he spoke harshly of some man who was not present. I ought to say that Lamb stuttered a little bit. And one of his friends said, "Why, Charles, I didn't know that you knew So-and-so?" "Oh," he said, "I don't. I can't hate a man I know."

There is a great deal of human nature, of very pleasant human nature, in that saying. It is hard to hate a man you know. I may admit, parenthetically, that there are some politicians whose methods I do not at all believe in, but they are jolly good fellows, and if they would not talk the wrong kind of politics with me I would love to be with them. And so it is all along the line, in serious matters and things less serious. We are all of the same clay and spirit, and we can get together if we desire to get together.

Therefore my counsel to you is this: Let us show ourselves Americans by showing that we do not want to go off in separate camps or groups by ourselves, but that we want to coöperate with all other classes and all other groups in a common enterprise, which is to release the spirits of the world from bondage. I would be willing to set that up as the final test of an American. That is the meaning of democracy.

We claim to be the greatest democratic people in the world, and democracy means, first of all, that we can govern ourselves. If our men have not self-control, then they are not capable of that great thing which we call democratic government. A man who takes the law into his own hands is not the right man to coöperate in any form of orderly development of law and institutions. And some of the processes by which the struggle between capital and labor is carried on are processes that come very near to taking the law into your own hands. I do not mean for a moment to compare them with what I have just been speaking of, but I want you to see that they are mere gradations of the manifestations of the unwillingness to coöperate. The fundamental lesson of the whole situation is that we must not only take common counsel, but that we must yield to and obey common counsel. Not all of the instrumentalities for this are at hand.

I am hopeful that in the very near future new instrumentalities may be organized by which we can see to it that various things that are now going on shall not go on. There are various processes of the dilution of labor and the unnecessary substitution of labor and bidding in different markets and unfairly upsetting the whole competition of labor which ought not to go on — I mean now, on the part of employers — and we must interject into this some instrumentality of coöperation by which the fair thing will be done all around.

I am hopeful that some such instrumentalities may be devised, but whether they are or not, we must use those that we have and upon every occasion where it is necessary have such an instrumentality originated upon that occasion, if necessary.

And so, my fellow-citizens, the reason that I came away from Washington is that I sometimes get lonely down there — there are so many people in Washington who know things that are not so, and there are so few people in Washington who know anything about what the people of the United States are thinking about. I have to come away to get reminded of the rest of the country. I have come away to talk to men who are up against the real thing and say to them, I am with you if you are with me. The only test of being with me is not to think about me personally at all, but merely to think of me as the expression for the time being of the power and dignity and hope of the American people.

THE KEEPERS OF THE LIGHT
THEODOSIA GARRISON

We are the keepers of that steadfast light
That guides a people's course and destiny;
Not ours the skill directing over the sea
The mighty beams that blaze the path aright:
Ours but the hands that, serving, keep it bright,
The bringers of the oil, the workers we
Who day long, without pause and faithfully,
Toil that its radiance may pierce the night.

Above us are the wills that guide and turn;
It is not ours to watch nor question these:
Ours but to see each wick is trimmed and fit,
Lest on a night of storm it fails to burn
And a Great Ship goes down in awful seas.
O Keepers of the light, keep faith with it!

A SONG OF SERVICE
THEODOSIA GARRISON

Folly and Complacency went singing through the dark,
They paused before a window that showed a candle's spark.

"Come forth, come forth and join us or bid us entrance win!"
"Nay, I've a wheel a-turning and I have wool to spin;
Unless your hands may aid me ye shall not enter in."

Folly and Complacency went singing through the night;
They paused before a casement that showed a shining light.
"Now bid us in, old Comrade, to revel until day!"
"Nay, I've a sword to sharpen to keep a foe at bay;
Unless your hands may aid me I speed you on your way."

Oh, there are swords to sharpen and there is wool to spin,
And woe betide the foolish ones who let these wastrels in!
At the cost of a dulled sword a people may be sold;
For lack of warmth a nation may perish in the cold,
And unto us the reckoning and price thereof be told.

Folly and Complacency — on our heads be the sin
If once our hands should slacken, our voices bid you in.
While there's a sword to sharpen, while there's a wheel to turn,
A word to say, a prayer to pray, a signal light to burn,
God give us strength and wakefulness to match the wage we earn.

MORE THAN A NAME[1]
SAMUEL GOMPERS

To me the term America is more than a name. It is more than a country. It is more than a continent. To me America is the apotheosis, a symbol of the ideas and the ideals for human betterment and human justice among the peoples of the world. Perhaps it may be strengthened by the hope, but somehow there is a sub-consciousness in me that tells me that when for the first time in the history of the world a Teutonic army shall face the soldiers of the United States with the flag, the Star-Spangled Banner, waving above them, it will penetrate the very souls of the men in the German uniform. In all their fights they have met men carrying the standards that Germany hated. They have never yet come in contact with Old Glory.

I ought to say, my friends, that the policy pursued by the government of the United States in this war, in matters of development and growth and preparation, amazes those who are permitted to know the truth. Some day, my friends, you and I, who may be kept from all the information just now, will know what marvels America has done within these past few months. And then, too, we have started out on a different line of action than in any previous wars in which we or any of the other countries on the globe have entered. It is to the honor of the committee of which I am chairman, that the bill was drafted which provides not only for compensation for injured soldiers and sailors and for their dependents, but

[1] From a speech delivered at Buffalo, September 14, 1917.

SAMUEL GOMPERS

also insurance, so that if any of the men come back injured they at least shall have the insurance to give them and their dependents an opportunity to live in some degree of comfort, and the opportunity of increasing their pay so that they can afford to lay something away as a nest-egg for themselves or to give to their families. We have tried to formulate a measure that shall relieve for all time the people of our country of the scandals and the injustice of the old pensions system, taking our experience as to the difference of the industrial and employers' liability acts and the substitution of compensation for workmen so as to apply it to the soldiers and the sailors of Uncle Sam. We hope that the boys who are already in France and the boys who are going over to France may have minds free from the worry that their families may possibly go down in the standard of life prevalent in their community. We want the boys of Uncle Sam fighting for us to feel that America, great America, will stand by them or those they may possibly leave behind them. And I am proud to say that that measure passed the House of Representatives yesterday by an almost unanimous vote.

We do not know now just exactly what sacrifices we may be called upon to make. Let us pray and hope and work that they may be few, if any at all; but this we feel assured of, from the President down to everyone aiding him and his in the great work of carrying on the war, it is the purpose that the home shall be maintained, that the standard of American life shall not go down, but shall be maintained throughout the war.

We must make it possible that our fighting force shall be provided with every necessity to fight and every means contributing to their subsistence and comfort, and that the American people shall go on in their economic, industrial, social and spiritual life just as well as it is possible to do; and so, when it is necessary to make additional sacrifices, we shall — you, and you, and you — the people of Chicago, the people of Illinois, the people of the United States, stand as one solid phalanx of the manhood and the womanhood of the people of our country, of our republic, united, determined to stand by our cause and our gallant allies until the world has been made safe for freedom, for justice, for democracy, for humanity.

WHAT THE STATE IS
SIR WILLIAM JONES

"What constitutes a state?
Not high-raised battlement or labored mound,
   Thick wall or moated gate;
Nor cities proud with spires and turrets crowned;
   Nor bays and broad-armed ports,
Where, laughing at the storm, rich navies ride;
   Not starred and spangled courts,
Where low-browed baseness wafts perfume to pride.
   No: — men, high-minded men,

   Men who their duties know,
But know their rights, and, knowing, dare maintain."

SOLDIERS OF FREEDOM
KATHARINE LEE BATES

They veiled their souls with laughter
    And many a mocking pose,
These lads who follow after
    Wherever Freedom goes;
These lads we used to censure
    For levity and ease,
On Freedom's high adventure
    Go shining overseas.

Our springing tears adore them,
    These boys at school and play,
Fair-fortuned years before them,
    Alas! but yesterday;
Divine with sudden splendor
    — Oh, how our eyes were blind! —
In careless self-surrender
    They battle for mankind.

Soldiers of Freedom! Gleaming
    And golden they depart,
Transfigured by the dreaming
    Of boyhood's hidden heart.
Her lovers they confess them
    And, rushing on her foes,
Toss her their youth — God bless them! —
    As lightly as a rose.

THE KHAKI
HENRY EDWARD WARNER

I

The khaki, the khaki! It flows in solid waves
Over the tops of shell holes, over the tops of graves,
Over the fields of Flanders, on to the Boche line —
And pride shall be behind them, and these hot tears of mine!
Tears for the heroes fallen, smiles for the men gone on,
Cheers for the stout, brave hearts of them who battle for the dawn —
The dawn of earth's new freedom! And we who watch and pray
Will grow our flowers for the wreaths of khaki sailed away!

II

The khaki, the khaki! O Thou who seest all,
Keep to the fore with khaki, and fend the shell and ball!
Strong in the might of virtue, strong for the newborn light
That signals freedom's coming day and scatters hopeless night.
The khaki, noble khaki, shall sweep o'er Flanders field,
Driving the hatred of the Hun until all hell shall yield!
And Thou who guidest planets — O Pilot of the soul! —
Thy voice shall give supreme command, Thy peace shall make us whole!

LESSONS OF THE WAR[1]
THEODORE ROOSEVELT

No man could fail to be thrilled by facing an audience like this, and I accept your greeting as not for me personally, but for the thing for which I stand — for Americanism, one flag, one country, and an undivided loyalty from every man and woman in this land.

We have a double right and double duty in connection with Americanism. On the one hand to suffer no discrimination against any man because of his birth or his creed, and on the other hand to insist that no man has a right to live in this country if he has any of Lot's wife attitude of looking back toward another country.

In the days of the Revolution we became a nation because Washington and the men who followed him in the field, and the men who signed the Declaration of Independence with him, because those men, although predominantly of English blood, stood straight against England and for America.

That lesson does not teach that we are to hate England. It is a mean and small soul who draws that lesson from it. That lesson teaches that we are to love liberty and to hate wrong, and stand for the right and against the wrong in each crisis as it comes up. The men of English descent in 1776 and in 1812 fought England because England was the foe of liberty and of America. And in just the same way we have a right to demand, not as a favor, but as a right, that every man of German descent now stand

---
[1] From the speech delivered at Dexter Pavilion, Chicago, September 8, 1918.

shoulder to shoulder with his fellow Americans against the bloody tyranny of the Prussianized autocracy of Germany.

And now in this country the events of the last three years will teach us much if we have the wit to read the lessons aright. There must be in this country one flag, only one flag, one allegiance, and only one allegiance, and one language, and that the language of the Declaration of Independence, of Washington's farewell address, of Lincoln's Gettysburg speech, and President Wilson's Message to Congress.

AMERICA RESURGENT

WENDELL PHILLIP STAFFORD

She is risen from the dead!
Loose the tongue and lift the head;
   Let the sons of light rejoice,
She has heard the challenge clear;
She has answered "I am here";
   She has made the stainless choice.

Bound with iron and with gold —
But her limbs they could not hold
   When the word of words was spoken;
Freedom calls —
The prison walls
   Tumble, and the bolts are broken!

Hail her! She is ours again —
Hope and heart of harassed men
   And the tyrants' doom and terror.

Send abroad the old alarms;
Call to arms, to arms, to arms,
    Hand of doubt and feet of error!

Cheer her! She is free at last,
With her back upon the past,
    With her feet upon the bars,
Hosts of freedom sorely prest,
Lo, a light is in the west
    And a helmet full of stars!

IN FORTY WEST

We are coming from the ranch; from the city and the mine,
And the word has gone before us to the town upon the Rhine;
    As the rising of the tide
    On the Old-World side,
We are coming to the battle, to the Line.

From the valleys of Virginia, from the Rockies in the North,
We are coming by battalions, for the word was carried forth:
    "We have put the pen away
    And the sword is out to-day,
For the Lord has loosed the Vintages of Wrath."

We are singing in the ships as they carry us to fight,
As our fathers sang before us by the camp-fires' light;
    In the wharf-light glare,
    They can hear us Over There,
When the ships come streaming through the night.

Right across the deep Atlantic where the *Lusitania* passed,
With the battle-flag of Yankee-land a-floating at the mast
    We are coming all the while,
    Over twenty hundred mile,
And we're staying to the finish, to the last.

We are many — we are one — and we're in it overhead,
We are coming as an army that has seen its women dead,
    And the old Rebel Yell
    Will be loud above the shell
When we cross the top together, seeing red.

—From *Blackwood's Magazine*

SOLDIERS ALL

DANIEL M. HENDERSON

"Fisherman, mend your nets
  For the day's trawling!
Cod and menhaden run
  Thick for your hauling!"
"*Yes, but beyond the mists
  Bugles are calling!*"

"Writer, the world would count
  You with its sages!
Far from the shock of war,
  Toil for the ages!"
"*No — I must write my life
  On Freedom's pages!*"

"Surgeon, *you* cannot go!
  Hear the sick pleading!
'T is not for such as you
  Bullets are speeding!"
"*Hush — for I see in France
  Liberty bleeding!*"

"Mother, keep back your lad,
  Tho his mates scorn him!
Better their jeers than that
  Your heart should mourn him!"
"*Cease — for his country's cause
  My arms have borne him!*"

"Pastor, now more and more
  Men need your preaching!
How shall they find their souls
  If you stop teaching?"
"*Yet, on His battle-line
  God is beseeching!*"

COMRADES IN A COMMON CAUSE[1]
BISHOP BRENT

We comrades in the common cause have come together like sturdy Judas Maccabæus and his fellow patriots in the ancient story, to commit our decision to the Lord and place ourselves in His hands before we pitch our camp and go forth to battle. It were an unworthy cause that we could not commit to God with complete confidence. Today we have this confidence.

This, I venture to say, is not merely the beginning of a new era, but of a new epoch. At this moment a great nation, well skilled in self-sacrifice, is standing by with deep sympathy and bidding Godspeed to another great nation that is making its act of self-dedication to God. That altar upon which we Americans are to-day laying our lives and our fortunes is already occupied. After three years Great Britain and her allies have been fighting not merely for their own laws, their own homes, their liberty, and all they hold sacred, but for the great commonwealth of mankind.

Today, when the United States avow their intention of giving themselves wholeheartedly to this great cause, the battle for the right assumes new proportions. A new power and victory — aye, a victory that is God's is in sight. We Americans have never been oblivious to the fact that the people of this country have been standing for the same principles which we love and for which we live. England, thank God, is the mother of democracy, and England's children come back today to pour all their

[1] From a speech delivered April 20th, 1917, in St. Paul's Cathedral, London.

Photo by Brown Bros

BISHOP BRENT

experience, the experience of a century and a half of independent life, with gratitude at the feet of their mother.

Today we stand side by side with our fellows as common soldiers in the common fight. There have been great quarrels in the past that were results of misunderstanding, but our quarrel with Germany is not based on misunderstanding. It is due to understanding. Just as it was understanding that made us break with Germany, so it is understanding which makes us take our place by the side of the Allies. It would have been impossible for us to do otherwise.

This act of America has enabled her to find her soul. America, which stands for democracy, must champion the cause of the plain people at all costs. The plain people most desire peace. That is what America with the Allies is fighting for. She thinks so much of peace that she is ready to pay the cost of war. Our war today is that we may destroy war. One thing to do with war is to hunt it to its death and, please God, in this war we shall achieve our purpose.

BRITONS AND GUESTS!
EDITH M. THOMAS

We fought you once — but that was long ago!
  We fought you once, O Briton hearts of oak;
    Away from you — from parent stock — we broke.
Be glad we did! Because from every blow
We hurled in that old day a force did grow
    That now shall stead you, level stroke by stroke —
  So Heaven help us, who but late awoke,
The charge upon our common race to know!

And we will stand with you, the world to save—
   To make it safe for Freedom (as we free have been)
Have you not seen our mutual banners wave
As one upon the wind—a sight most brave! . . .
   We once did fight you ev'n as next of kin
May cleave apart, at end to closer win!

CHRIST IN FLANDERS
A BRITISH SOLDIER

We had forgotten You or very nearly,
You did not seem to touch us very nearly.
   Of course we thought about You now and then
Especially in any time of trouble,
We know that You were good in time of trouble
   But we are very ordinary men.

And there were always other things to think of,
There's lots of things a man has got to think of,
   His work, his home, his pleasure and his wife,
And so we only thought of You on Sunday;
Sometimes perhaps not even on a Sunday
   Because there's always lots to fill one's life.

And all the while, in street or lane or byway
In country lane, in city street or byway
   You walked among us, and we did not see.
Your feet were bleeding, as You walked our pavements
How did we miss Your foot-prints on our pavements:
   Can there be other folk as blind as we?

Now we remember over here in Flanders
(It isn't strange to think of You in Flanders)
   This hideous warfare seems to make things clear,

We never thought about You much in England
But now that we are far away from England
   We have no doubts—we *know* that You are *here*.

You helped us pass the jest along the trenches
Where, in cold blood, we waited in the trenches,
   You touched its ribaldry and made it fine.
You stood beside us in our pain and weakness.
We're glad to think You understand our weakness.
   Somehow it seems to help us not to whine.

We think about You kneeling in the Garden—
Ah! God, the agony of that dread Garden;
   We know you prayed for us upon the Cross.
If anything could make us glad to bear it
'Twould be the knowledge, that You willed to bear it—
   Pain, death, the uttermost of human loss.

Tho' we forgot You, You will not forget us.
We feel so sure that You will not forget us,
   But stay with us until this dream is past—
And so we ask for courage, strength, and pardon,
Especially I think, we ask for pardon,
   And that You'll stand beside us to the last.

ONWARD, CHRISTIAN SOLDIERS
S. BARING-GOULD

   Onward, Christian soldiers,
     Marching as to war;
   With the cross of Jesus
     Going on before.

Christ, the royal Master,
　Leads against the foe:
Forward into battle,
　See, His banners go.

Like a mighty army
　Moves the Church of God;
Brothers, we are treading
　Where the saints have trod;
We are not divided,
　All one body we,
One in hope and doctrine,
　One in charity.

Crowns and thrones may perish,
　Kingdoms wax and wane,
But the Church of Jesus
　Constant will remain;
Gates of hell can never
　'Gainst that Church prevail;
We have Christ's own promise,
　And that cannot fail.

Onward, then, ye people,
　Join our happy throng;
Blend with ours your voices
　In the triumph-song;
Glory, laud, and honor,
　Unto Christ the King;
This through countless ages
　Men and angels sing.

ENGLAND'S CASE
HERBERT H. ASQUITH

The War which is now shaking to its foundations the whole European system originated in a quarrel in which this country had no direct concern. We strove with all our might to prevent its outbreak, and when that was no longer possible, to limit its area. It is all important that it should be clearly understood when and why it was that we intervened. It was only when we were confronted with the choice between keeping and breaking solemn obligations, between the discharge of a binding trust and of shameless subservience to naked force, that we threw away the scabbard. We do not repent our decision. The issue was one which no great and self-respecting nation, certainly none bred and nurtured like ourselves, in this ancient home of liberty, could, without undying shame, have declined. We were bound by our obligations, plain and paramount, to assert and maintain the threatened independence of a small and neutral state. Belgium had no interests of her own to serve, save and except the one supreme and ever-widening interest of every state, great or little, which is worthy of the name, the preservation of her integrity and of her national life.

CANADA TO ENGLAND
WILFRED CAMPBELL

England, England, England,
  Girdled by ocean and skies,
And the power of a world, and the heart of a race,
  And a hope that never dies!

England, England, England,
  Wherever a true heart beats,
Wherever the armies of commerce flow,
Wherever the bugles of conquest blow,
Wherever the glories of liberty grow,
  'T is the name that the world repeats.

  *   *   *

North and South and East and West,
  Wherever their triumphs be,
Their glory goes home to the ocean-girt Isle
Where the heather blooms and the roses smile,
  With the green Isle under her lee.
And if ever the smoke of an alien gun
  Should threaten her iron repose,
Shoulder to shoulder against the world,
  Face to face with her foes,
Scot and Celt and Saxon are one,
  Where the glory of England goes.

  *   *   *

Till the last great freedom is found,
  And the last great truth be taught,
Till the last great deed be done,
  And the last great battle is fought;
Till the last great fighter is slain in the last great fight
  And the war-wolf is dead in his den,
England, breeder of hope and valour and might,
  Iron mother of men!

Yea, England, England, England,
  Till honour and valour are dead,
Till the world's great cannons rust,
Till the world's great hopes are dust,
  Till faith and freedom be fled:

Till wisdom and justice have passed
To sleep with those who sleep in the many-chambered
   vast,
Till glory and knowledge are charnelled, dust in dust,
To all that is best in the world's unrest
   In heart and mind you are wed:—

While out from the Indian jungle
   To the far Canadian snows,
Over the east and over the west,
Over the worst and over the best,
The flag of the world to its winds unfurled,
   The blood-red ensign blows.

AUSTRALIA TO ENGLAND
ARCHIBALD T. STRONG

By all the deeds to thy dear glory done,
   By all the life blood spilt to serve thy need,
   By all the fettered lives thy touch hath freed,
By all thy dream in us anew begun;
By all the guerdon English sire to son
   Hath given of highest vision, kingliest deed,
   By all thine agony, of God decreed
For trial and strength, our fate with thine is one.

Still dwells thy spirit in our hearts and lips,
   Honour and life we hold from none but thee,
   And if we live thy pensioners no more
But seek a nation's might of men and ships,
   'T is but that when the world is black with war
Thy sons may stand beside thee strong and free.

INDIA TO ENGLAND
NIZAMAT JUNG

O England! in thine hour of need,
When Faith's reward and valor's meed
  Is death or glory,
When Faith indites, with biting brand,
Clasped in each warrior's stiffening hand,
  A nation's story;

Though weak our hands, which fain would clasp
The warrior's sword with warrior's grasp
  On victory's field;
Yet turn, O mighty Mother! turn
Unto the million hearts that burn
  To be thy shield.

Thine equal justice, mercy, grace
Have made a distant alien race
  A part of thee.
'T was thine to bid their souls rejoice
When first they heard the living voice
  Of Liberty.

Unmindful of their ancient name,
And lost to honor — glory — fame,
  And sunk in strife,
Thou found them, whom thy touch hath made
Men, and to whom thy breath conveyed
  A nobler life.

They, whom thy love hath guarded long;
They, whom thy care hath rendered strong
  In love and faith.

Their heartstrings round thy heart entwine,
They are, they ever will be, thine
In life — in death.

A MESSAGE TO IRELAND

FLORENCE GOFF

Listen, I'm writin' ye, Jimmy O'Flanigan,
  Sindin' a message from over the seas;
Shame to ould Ireland and all of her fightin' men!
  Faith, 't is no time to go weak in the knees.

Shades of St. Patrick, but I must confess to ye,
  Much as I love the ould Emerald sod,
I, Mike O'Brien, am wishin' bad cess to ye
  Shirkin' your duty to freedom and God.

Quit your shenanigan, with the world riotin';
  Sure 't is an Irishman's time to fall in;
When the war's over thin talk about quietin'
  England's oppression, but now 't is a sin.

Faith, 't is the Kaiser himself would be rulin' ye.
  Niver swap horses whin crossin' a stream;
Turn a deaf ear to the traitor that's foolin' ye,
  Jimmy, belave me, 't is no idle dream.

Here in America, where they are feedin' us,
  Faith, there are men that the devil can't scare;
Ready to wallop the brute that is bleedin' us,
  Ready to follow — the devil knows where.

Shame to ye, shame to ye, Jimmy O'Flanigan,
  Roustin' conscription. Come on wid the b'ys;
Let the ould Kaiser know Paddy's a man agin;
  Sure 't is ould Ireland can blacken his eyes.

GOING HOME
ROBERT W. SERVICE

I'm goin' 'ome to Blighty — ain't I glad to 'ave the chance!
I'm loaded up wiv fightin', and I've 'ad my fill o' France;
I'm feelin' so excited-like, I want to sing and dance,
  For I'm goin' 'ome to Blighty in the mawnin'.

I'm goin' 'ome to Blighty; can you wonder as I'm gay?
I've got a wound I would n't sell for 'alf a year o' pay —
A harm that's smashed to jelly in the nicest sort o' way,
  For it takes me 'ome to Blighty in the mawnin'.

'Ow everlastin' keen I was on gettin' to the front!
I'd ginger for á dozen, and I 'elped to bear the brunt;
But Cheese and Crust! I'm crazy, now I've done me little stunt,
  To sniff the air of Blighty in the mawnin'.

I've looked upon the wine that's white and on the wine that's red;
I've looked on cider flowin', till it fairly turned me 'ead;
But oh, the finest scoff will be, when all is done and said,
  A pint o' Bass in Blighty in the mawnin'.

I'm goin' back to Blighty, which I left to strafe the 'Un;
I've fought in bloody battles, and I've 'ad a 'eap of fun;

GOING HOME

But now me flipper's busted, and I think me dooty's done,
And I'll kiss me gel in Blighty in the mawnin'.

Oh, there be furrin' lands to see, and some of 'em be fine,
And there be furrin' gels to kiss, and scented furrin' wine;
But there's no land like England, and no other gel like mine.
Thank Gawd for dear old Blighty in the mawnin'.

CANADA STANDS FAST[1]
SIR ROBERT LAIRD BORDEN

I am proud of the part that Canada has played in this war. It was due to the fact that her sons stood in the way that the path to Calais was not opened. We were a peaceful people, absorbed in the peaceful vocations of life before the outbreak of this war; but we have since proved that when the call came to fight we were ready and willing to respond.

And now that we have made great sacrifices and have sent our sons to the defense of the Empire, there is one thing that I desire to say to you: Canada is as determined to maintain the cause to the end as it was when this war began. While we all pray for peace and hope that it be not long deferred, so long as we in Canada have a voice there will be no truce, nor an inconclusive peace.

Something depends on the principles for which this war has been fought, and we in Canada believe that all our sacrifices will have been in vain unless these principles, the principles for which we have fought, principles for civilization and right, as we understand them, are maintained and are made triumphant. If those principles are maintained we will emerge from the war purified and triumphant. But if it is to mean only a truce and a preparation for another war, then, as far as we are concerned, it were much better that we had never fought at all.

We have fought for certain principles and we mean to maintain them to the end. Last week I looked into the keen, intent faces of 10,000 Canadian soldiers within

---
[1] From speeches delivered by Sir Robert Laird Borden.

Sir Robert Laird Borden

sound and range of the German guns. Three days ago I looked into the undaunted eyes of 1,000 Canadian convalescents returned from the valley of the shadow of death. In the eyes and in the faces of those men I read only one message, that of resolute and unflinching determination to make our cause triumphant, to preserve our institutions and our liberties, to maintain the unity of our Empire and its influence through the world. That message I bring to you also from the great Dominion which has sent those men across the sea. While the awful shadow of this war overhangs our Empire I shall not pause to speak of what may be evolved in its constitutional relations. Upon what has been built in the past, it is possible, in my judgment, that an even nobler and more enduring fabric may be erected. That structure must embody the autonomy of the self-governing Dominions and of the British Isles as well, but it must embody also the majesty and power of an Empire, and be more thoroughly and effectively organized for the purpose of preserving its own existence.

TO CANADA

KATHARINE LEE BATES

Our neighbor of the undefended bound,
    Friend of the hundred years of peace, our kin,
Fellow adventurer on the enchanted ground
    Of the New World, must not the pain within
Our hearts for this vast anguish of the war
    Be keenest for your pain? Is not our grief,

That aches with all bereavement, tenderest for
  The tragic crimson on your maple-leaf?

Bitter our lot, in this world-clash of faiths,
  To stand aloof and bide our hour to serve;
The glorious dead are living; we are wraiths,
  Dim watchers of the conflict's changing curve,
Yet proud for human valor, spirit true
  In scorn of body, manhood on the crest
Of consecration, dearly proud for you,
  Who sped to arms like knighthood to the quest

From quaint Quebec to stately Montreal,
  Along the rich St. Lawrence, o'er the steep
Roofs of the Rockies rang the bugle-call,
  And east and west, deep answering to deep,
Your sons surged forth, the simple, stooping folk
  Of shop and wheatfield sprung to hero size
Swiftly as e'er your northern lights awoke
  To streaming splendor quiet evening skies.

Seek not your lost beneath the tortured sod
  Of France and Flanders, where in desperate strife
They battled greatly for the cause of God;
  But when above the snow your heavens are rife
With those upleaping lustres, find them there,
  Ardors of sacrifice, celestial sign,
Aureole your angel shall forever wear,
  Praising the irresistible Divine.

A CRY FROM THE CANADIAN HILLS

LILIAN LEVERIDGE

Laddie, little laddie, come with me over the hills,
Where blossom the white May lilies, and the dogwood and daffodils;
For the Spirit of Spring is calling to our spirits that love to roam
Over the hills of home, laddie, over the hills of home.

Laddie, little laddie, here's hazel and meadow rue,
And wreaths of the rare arbutus, a-blowing for me and you;
And cherry and bilberry blossoms, and hawthorn as white as foam,
We'll carry them all to Mother, laddie, over the hills at home.

Laddie, little laddie, the winds have many a song,
And blithely and bold they whistle to us as we trip along;
But your own little song is sweeter, your own with its merry trills;
So, whistle a tune as you go, laddie, over the windy hills.

Laddie, little laddie, 'tis time that the cows were home,
Can you hear the klingle-klangle of their bell in the greenwood gloam?
Old Rover is waiting, eager to follow the trail with you,
Whistle a tune as you go, laddie, whistle a tune as you go.

Laddie, little laddie, there's a flash of a bluebird's wing.
O hush! If we wait and listen we may hear him caroling.

The vesper song of the thrushes, and the plaint of the whip-poor-wills,
Sweet, how sweet is the music, laddie, over the twilit hills.

Brother, little brother, your childhood is passing by,
And the dawn of a noble purpose I see in your thoughtful eye.
You have many a mile to travel and many a task to do;
Whistle a tune as you go, laddie, whistle a tune as you go.

Laddie, soldier laddie, a call comes over the sea,
A call to the best and bravest in the land of liberty,
To shatter the despot's power, to lift up the weak that fall.
Whistle a song as you go, laddie, to answer your country's call.

Brother, soldier brother, the Spring has come back again,
But her voice from the windy hilltops is calling your name in vain;
For never shall we together 'mid the birds and the blossoms roam,
Over the hills of home, brother, over the hills of home.

Laddie! Laddie! Laddie! "Somewhere in France" you sleep,
Somewhere 'neath alien flowers and alien winds that weep.
Bravely you marched to battle, nobly your life laid down,
You unto death were faithful, laddie; yours is the victor's crown.

Laddie! Laddie! Laddie! How dim is the sunshine grown,
As Mother and I together speak softly in tender tone!

And the lips that quiver and falter have ever a single
   theme,
As we list for your dear, lost whistle, laddie, over the
   hills of dream.

Laddie, beloved laddie! How soon should we cease to
   weep
Could we glance through the golden gateway whose keys
   the angels keep!
Yet love, our love that is deathless, can follow you where
   you roam,
Over the hills of God, laddie, the beautiful hills of Home.

THE RECKONING
THEODORE GOODRIDGE ROBERTS

Ye who reckon with England —
   Ye who sweep the seas
Of the flag that Rodney nailed aloft
   And Nelson flung to the breeze —
Count well your ships and your men,
   Count well your horse and your guns,
For they who reckon with England
   Must reckon with England's sons.

Ye who would challenge England —
   Ye who would break the might
Of the little isle in the foggy sea
   And the lion-heart in the fight —
Count well your horse and your swords,
   Weigh well your valour and guns,
For they who would ride against England
   Must sabre her million sons.

THE SPIRIT OF DEMOCRACY

Ye who would roll to warfare
    Your hordes of peasants and slaves,
To crush the pride of an empire
    And sink her fame in the waves —
Test well your blood and your mettle,
    Count well your troops and your guns
For they who battle with England
    Must war with a Mother's sons.

A LEAGUE OF NATIONS[1]
WOODROW WILSON

We are participants, whether we would or not, in the life of the world. The interests of all nations are our own also. We are partners with the rest. What affects mankind is inevitably our affair as well as the affair of the nations of Europe and of Asia.

Only when the great nations of the world have reached some sort of agreement as to what they hold to be fundamental to their common interest, and as to some feasible method of acting in concert when any nation or group of nations seeks to disturb those fundamental things, can we feel that civilization is at last in a way of justifying its existence and claiming to be finally established. It is clear that nations must in the future be governed by the same high code of honor that we demand of individuals.

Repeated utterances of the leading statesmen of most of the great nations now engaged in war have made it plain that their thought has come to this, that the principle of public right must henceforth take precedence over the individual interests of particular nations, and that the nations of the world must in some way band themselves together to see that right prevails as against any sort of selfish aggression; that henceforth alliance must not be set up against alliance, understanding against understanding, but that there must be a common agreement for a common object, and that at the heart of that common object must lie the inviolable rights of peoples and of mankind.

---
[1] From an address to the League to Enforce Peace, Washington, D. C.

The nations of the world have become each other's neighbors. It is to their interest that they should understand each other. In order that they may understand each other it is imperative that they should agree to cooperate in a common cause, and that they should so act that the guiding principle of that common cause shall be even-handed and impartial justice.

If it should ever be our privilege to suggest or initiate a movement for peace among the nations now at war, I am sure that the people of the United States would wish their Government to move along these lines:

First such a settlement with regard to their own immediate interests as the belligerents may agree upon. We have nothing material of any kind to ask for ourselves, and we are in no sense or degree parties to the present quarrel. Our interest is only in peace and its future guarantees.

Second, an universal association of the nations to maintain the inviolate security of the highway of the seas for the common and unhindered use of all the nations of the world, and to prevent any war begun contrary to treaty covenants or without warning and full submission of the causes to the opinion of the world—a virtual guarantee of territorial integrity and political independence.

A PRAYER IN TIME OF WAR
ALFRED NOYES

Thou, whose deep ways are in the sea,
    Whose footsteps are not known,
Tonight a world that turned from Thee
    Is waiting—at Thy Throne.

The towering Babels that we raised
  Where scoffing sophists brawl,
The little Antichrists we praised —
  The night is on them all.

The fool hath said . . . The fool hath said . .
  And we, who deemed him wise,
We who believed that Thou wast dead,
  How should we seek Thine eyes?

How should we seek to Thee for power
  Who scorned Thee yesterday?
How should we kneel, in this dread hour?
  Lord, teach us how to pray!

Grant us the single heart, once more,
  That mocks no sacred thing,
The Sword of Truth our fathers wore
  When Thou wast Lord and King.

Let darkness unto darkness tell
  Our deep unspoken prayer,
For, while our souls in darkness dwell,
  We know that Thou art there.

AMERICA TO FRANCE AND GREAT BRITAIN
HAROLD T. PULSIFER
MASTER SIGNAL ELECTRICIAN, SIGNAL CORPS, U. S. N. A.

France! Britain! to your stalwart sons
We owe our hearthstones undefiled,
Our living cities: — to your guns
The laughter of each little child.

France! Britain! in the deadly pall
That hangs athwart your eastern skies,
We see the measure of our call,
The need of holy sacrifice.

France! Britain! in your debt we stand
As never nation stood before,—
Henceforth the honor of our land
Speaks only where our cannons roar.

In gilded word and burnished phrase
There is no balm for blood that flows
From those who through infernal days
Fight liberty's eternal foes.

Before the judgment seat of God
Ten thousand hopes will not outweigh
One single square of bloody sod
Held from the Hun in red affray.

Late to the battlefield we come
Unready, tortured with the shame
Of seeing brothers grim and dumb
Dying,—where we should feel the flame.

France! Britain! when the stars look down
Upon the last great battle place,
Pray God we may have won our crown, —
The right to meet you face to face!

THE CHALLENGE

H. T. SUDDRITH

Across the sea a challenge came
With roar of guns and flash of flame!
'Twixt Might and Right the line was drawn
And freedom's last great fight was on!
America that challenge heard!
Her answer all the world has stirred!
See! Streaming on the winds of France
Her flag and allied flags advance!
Nor will those allied flags be furled
Till freedom triumphs through the world.

THE HOLY QUEST[1]
RABBI STEPHEN S. WISE

There are those who openly mock or grimly smile at our national program, maintaining that the end of this war is bound to be evil, not only because war ever brings curses in its train, but because we are certain to surrender some of the most precious gains of the democratic life, howbeit we have set forth to overwhelm them that are democracy's foes. I do not so believe, for my own is too great a trust in the power of my countrymen to achieve their purposes. We have set out upon a high and holy quest. We will not basely stoop in our pursuit thereof. We who enter the war without intent to do evil but rather to release them that are in bondage shall not so falter as to enthrall ourselves. If we can war without hatred of the enemy, can we not triumph without hurt to ourselves? We will no more than to serve the world and not to disserve ourselves through deserting the ideals which are the soul of America.

Yet another reason there is for resolving that we shall not lose America as we strive to win the war. The war must and will be won by them who are ready to lay down their life to the end that victory may crown our arms. Whilst these set forth to win the war, dare we do less than determine that the aims of America on behalf of which they wage war, on behalf of which they are ready to dare and to die, shall not be defeated at home whilst through their service and sacrifice its arms triumph abroad? Whilst these sacrifice themselves for America,

---
[1] From an address delivered in 1917 in the Free Synagogue, NewYork

RABBI STEPHEN S. WISE

we must not sacrifice America on any ground whatsoever. We ask the young men of America to win the war. Let it not become needful for them to demand of us that we, who are to live amid security because of their service and their sacrifice, shall not lose their and our America.

Not very long ago, I was asked to have part in a "Wake Up America" demonstration from which I absented myself because tawdryness and vulgarity have no part in our international strife. The methods of the circus ring ought not to be associated even remotely with the most sombre event in human history. Wake Up America!— not only to the need of hard fighting which is inevitable, but the duty of preserving inviolate the high aims of this war. Wake Up America!— and wage a war without hatred, without bitterness, without vindictiveness, a war without indemnity exacted from others outwardly or from ourselves inwardly.

Wake Up America to the nobleness of our part in the strife not for profit to ourselves nor yet for punishment of others, but for the liberation of all peoples, including above all the liberation of the peoples of the German Empire from Cæsarism.

Wake Up America!—to the greatness and the nobleness of our quest, the making secure forever of the sanctity of international covenant and the rights of smaller nations, of democracy for all the world.

Wake Up America and win the war for the world, but hold and keep holy America's soul.

HANDS ALL ROUND
ALFRED TENNYSON

*   *   *   *

Gigantic daughter of the West,
    We drink to thee across the flood,
We know thee and we love thee best,
    For art thou not of British blood?
Should war's mad blast again be blown,
    Permit not thou the tyrant powers
To fight thy mother here alone,
    But let thy broadsides roar with ours.
          Hands all round!
    God the tyrant's cause confound!
To our dear kinsmen of the West, my friends,
    And the great name of England, round and round

O rise, our strong Atlantic sons,
    When war against our freedom springs!
O speak to Europe through your guns!
    They *can* be understood by kings.
You must not mix our Queen with those
    That wish to keep their people fools;
Our freedom's foemen are her foes,
    She comprehends the race she rules.
          Hands all round!
    God the tyrant's cause confound!
To our dear kinsmen in the West, my friends,
    And the great name of England, round and round.

CARRY ON!

JOHN OXENHAM

"Carry on, Brave Hearts! Carry on!" —
Rings, like a clarion cry,
Our heart-felt valedictory,
To cheer you on to victory; —
  "Carry on, Brave Hearts! Carry on!"
Now bear you well, and bear you high,
Who fights for God to God draws nigh,
And wins him immortality; —
  "Carry on, Brave Hearts! Carry on!"

The night is past, day dawns at last; —
  "Carry on, Brave Hearts! Carry on!"

The way is clear, the goal is near; —
  "Carry on, Brave Hearts! Carry on!"

God's Best awaits beyond these straits; —
  "Carry on, Brave Hearts! Carry on!"

For Peace on Earth is at the birth; —
  "Carry on, Brave Hearts! Carry on!"

The fateful day is all your own,
The Evil Thing is overthrown,
The mighty victory is won; —
  "Carry on, Brave Hearts! Carry on!"
Your might shall set Christ on His Throne,
And His sweet grace in full atone
For all that you have undergone; —
  "Carry on, Brave Hearts! Carry on!"

TO THE UNITED STATES OF AMERICA
ROBERT BRIDGES

Brothers in blood! They who this wrong began
  To wreck our commonwealth, will rue the day
  When first they challenged freemen to the fray,
And with the Briton dared the American.
Now are we pledged to win the Rights of man;
  Labour and Justice now shall have their way,
  And in a League of Peace — God grant we may —
Transform the earth, not patch up the old plan.

Sure is our hope since he who led your nation
  Spake for mankind, and ye arose in awe
Of that high call to work the world's salvation;
  Clearing your minds of all estranging blindness
  In the vision of Beauty and the Spirit's law,
    Freedom and Honour and sweet Lovingkindness

THE WESTERN LAND
CAROLINE HAZARD

Great Western Land whose mighty breast
Between two oceans finds its rest,
Begirt with storm on either side,
And washed by strong Pacific tide;
The knowledge of thy wondrous birth
Gave balance to the rounded earth,
In sea of darkness thou didst stand
Now first in light, my Western land.

In thee the olive and the vine
Unite with hemlock and with pine;

THE WESTERN LAND

In purest white the Southern rose
Repeats the spotless Northern snows.
Around thy zone the belt of maize
Rejoices in the sun's hot rays,
And all that Nature could command
She heaped on thee, my Western land.

My Western land, whose touch makes free,
Advance to perfect liberty!
Till right shall make thy sovereign might,
And every wrong be crushed from sight.
Behold thy day, thy time is here,
Thy people great, with naught to fear,
God hold thee in His strong right hand,
My well beloved Western land.

A MESSAGE TO AMERICA[1]
ROMAIN ROLLAND

My faith is great in the high destinies of America. And it is clear to me that the events of today make more urgent than before that these be realized. On our old Continent, civilization is menaced. It becomes America's solemn duty to uphold the wavering torch.

You have great advantages over the European nations. You are free of traditions. You are free of that vast load of thought, of sentiment, of secular obsession under which the Old World groans. The intellectual fixed ideas, the dogmas of politics and art that grip us, are unknown to you. You may go forward, unhampered, to your future; while we, in Europe, sacrifice ours, daily, to quarrels and rancors and ambitions that should be dead. Europe has found no better channel for its genius than to revive these quarrels; to submit, over and again, to the tyrannies that they impose. And each time that Europe attempts to solve them, it succeeds merely in strengthening the web that binds it. Where it should strike clear of its shackles, it forges still more iron meshes. Like the *Atrides*, it works out its tragedy under a curse. And like them, again, it prays for its release in vain, to some indifferent god.

In conclusion, writers and thinkers of America, we expect of you two things. We ask that you defend the cause of Liberty; that you defend its conquests; and that you increase them. And by Liberty I mean both political and intellectual liberty. I mean the incessant rebirth

---
[1] From an address delivered in 1917.

Photo by Brown Bros.

ROMAIN ROLLAND

and replenishment of life that it enfolds. I mean the wide River of Spirit that never stagnates, but flows on forever.

Also, we ask that you so master your lives as to give to the world a new ideal for lack of which it bleeds—an ideal, not of section and tradition, but of Harmony. You must harmonize all of the dreams and liberties and thoughts brought to your shores by all your peoples. You must make of your culture a symphony that shall in a true way express your brotherhood of individuals, of races, of cultures banded together. You must make real the dream of an integrated entire humanity.

You are fortunate. Your life is young and abundant. Your land is vast and free for the discovery of your works. You are at the beginning of your journey, at the dawn of your day. There is in you no weariness of the Yesterdays; no clutterings of the Past.

Behind you, alone, the elemental Voice of a great pioneer, in whose message you may well find an almost legendary omen of your task to come —your Homer: Walt Whitman.

Surge et Age [Rise and Act].

AMERICA THE BEAUTIFUL
KATHARINE LEE BATES

O beautiful for spacious skies,
    For amber waves of grain,
For purple mountain majesties
    Above the fruited plain!

America! America!
God shed His grace on thee
And crown thy good with brotherhood
From sea to shining sea!

O beautiful for pilgrim feet,
Whose stern, impassioned stress
A thoroughfare for freedom beat
Across the wilderness!
America! America!
God mend thine every flaw,
Confirm thy soul in self-control,
Thy liberty in law!

O beautiful for heroes proved
In liberating strife,
Who more than self their country loved
And mercy more than life!
America! America!
May God thy gold refine,
Till all success be nobleness,
And every gain divine!

O beautiful for patriot dream
That sees beyond the years
Thine alabaster cities gleam
Undimmed by human tears!
America! America!
God shed His grace on thee
And crown thy good with brotherhood
From sea to shining sea!

WE SHALL REMEMBER THEM
JAMES TERRY WHITE

They sleep beneath no immemorial yews;
  Their resting place no temple arches hem;
No blazoned shaft or graven tablet woos
  Men's praise — and yet, we shall remember them.

The unforgetting clouds shall drop their tears;
  The winds, in ceaseless lamentation, wail,
For God's white Knights are lying on their biers,
  Who pledged their service to restore the Grail.

They gave their lives to make the whole world free;
  They recked not to what flag they were assigned;
The starry Banner, Cross, or Fleur-de-lis —
  Their sacrifice was made for all mankind.

For them the task is done, the strife is stilled;
  No more shall care disturb, nor zeal condemn;
And when the larger good has been fulfilled,
  In coming years we shall remember them.

How can the world their deeds forget? In France
  White crosses everywhere lift pallid hands,
Like silent sentinels with sword and lance,
  To keep their memory safe for other lands.

What need have they for holy sepulture?
  Within the hearts of men is hallowed ground —
A sanctuary where they rest secure,
  And with Love's immortality are crowned.

And far-off voices of the future sing,
  "They shall remain in memory's diadem";
And winds of promise still are whispering
  That same refrain. "We shall remember them."

KEEP THE ROAD OF DEMOCRACY OPEN[1]
WILLIAM E. BORAH

What we have determined in this crisis, as I understand it, is that we will keep the road of democracy open. No one shall close it. If any nation shall hereafter rise to the sublime requirement of self-government and choose to go that way, it shall have the right to do so. Above all things we have determined, cost what it may in treasure and blood, that this experiment here upon this Western Continent shall justify the faith of its builders, that there shall remain here in all the integrity of its powers, neither wrenched nor marred by the passions of war from within nor humbled nor dishonored by military power from without, the Republic of the fathers; that since the challenge has been thrown down that this is a war unto death between two opposing theories of government we are determined that whatever else happens as a result of this war this form of organization, this theory of state, this last great hope, this fruition of one hundred thirty years of struggle and toil, "shall not perish from the earth."

We can and should keep the issue clear of all selfish and imperialistic ambitions, but the issue itself cannot be compromised. Cost what it may in treasure and blood, the burden, as if by fate, has been laid upon us, and we must meet it manfully and successfully. To compromise is to acknowledge defeat. The policies of Frederick the Great which would make of all human souls mere cogs in a vast military machine, and the policies of Washington which would make government the expression and the

[1] From a speech delivered March 18, 1918.

instrument of popular power are contending for supremacy on the battlefields of Europe. Just that single, simple, stupendous issue, beside which all other issues in this war are trivial, must have a settlement as clear and conclusive as the settlement at Runnymede or Yorktown. To lose sight of this fact is to miss the supreme purpose of the war, and to permit it to be embarrassed or belittled by questions of territory is to betray the cause of civilization. And to fail to settle it clearly and conclusively is to fail in the most vital and sublime task ever laid upon a people.

We need not prophesy now when victory will come. Neither is it profitable to speculate how it will come. If it is a real and not a sham peace, we will have no trouble in recognizing it when it does come. Whether it shall come in the bloody and visible triumph of arms or, as we hope, through the overthrow and destruction of militarism by the people of the respective countries, we do not know. But that it will come we most confidently believe. Indeed, if the principles of right and the precepts of liberty are not a myth, we know it will come.

It has been said by some one that it was not possible for Napoleon to win at Waterloo, not on account of Wellington, not on account of Bluecher, but on account of the unchanging laws of liberty and justice. Let us call something of this faith to our own contest. Let us go forward in the belief that it is not possible in the morning of the twentieth century of the Christian civilization for militarism, for brute force, to triumph.

We cannot lose. We must win. The only question is whether we shall, through efficiency and concerted action, win without unnecessary loss of life, unnecessary waste of treasure, or whether we shall, through lack of unity in spirit and purpose, win only after fearful and unnecessary sacrifices.

It has often been said since the war began that a republic cannot make war. I trample the doctrine under my feet. I scorn the faithless creed as the creed of cowards and traitors. A republic can make war. It can make war successfully and triumphantly and remain a republic every hour of the conflict. The genius who presided over the organization of this Republic, whose impressive force was knit into every fibre of our national organization, knew that though devoted to peace the time would come when the Republic would have to make war. Over and over again he solemnly warned his countrymen to be ever ready and always prepared. He intended, therefore, that this Republic should make war and make war effectively, and the Republic which Washington framed and baptized with his love can make war. Let these faithless recreants cease to preach their pernicious doctrine.

This theory, this belief that a self-governing people cannot make war without forfeiting their freedom and their form of government is vicious enough to have been kenneled in some foreign clime. A hundred million people knit together by the ties of a common patriotism, united in spirit and purpose, conscious of the fact that their freedom is imperiled, and exerting their energies and asserting their powers through the avenues and machinery of a representative Republic is the most masterful enginery of war yet devised by man. It has in it a power, an element of strength, which no military power of itself can bring into effect.

The American soldier, a part of the life of his nation, imbued with devotion to his country, has something in him that no system of mere military training and discipline as applied to automatons of an absolute Government can ever give. The most priceless heritage which this war will leave to a war-torn and weary world is the demonstrated fact that a free people of a free Government can make war successfully and triumphantly, can defy and defeat militarism and preserve through it all their independence, their freedom, and the integrity of their institutions.

RESURREXIT
(Paris, Easter, 1917)
GRACE ELLERY CHANNING

"Three days and nights" they watched their sleeping Lord:
But we — three years of days
We have not taken our hands off from the sword,
Nor our eyes from her face.
Others might sleep: we loving most, have kept
Vigil stern soldiers keep:
The terror walked in darkness, and She slept
When it was death to sleep,—
When it was shame.
We have not ceased to call upon her name,
To watch — to fight — to pray;
Now let her late-awakened take our place;
Yes, let them have their day,
And we our sleep;
We have not slept, so long, for her love's sake,
But now — she is awake,
Awake: and all her stars point out the way!

Sleep — did I say?
Rather our eyes shall their full rapture take,
Nor yet the full heart break
Beholding how her Angel rolls away
The years of our despair,
And at her first word uttered on the air,
How the glad, generous nations run to greet
Her coming hands and feet.
What matters now what mortal griefs may come,
What agonies to bear —
When Freedom's brightest armies shall turn home
She will be marching there!

THE ROAD TO FRANCE
DANIEL M. HENDERSON

Thank God our liberating lance
Goes flaming on the way to France!
To France — the trail the Gurkhas found!
To France — old England's rallying ground
To France — the path the Russians strode!
To France — the Anzacs' glory road!
To France — where our Lost Legion ran
To fight and die for God and Man!
To France — with every race and breed
That hates Oppression's brutal creed!

Ah, France — how could our hearts forget
The path by which came Lafayette?
How could the haze of doubt hang low
Upon the road to Rochambeau?
How was it that we missed the way
Brave Joffre leads us along to-day?
At last, thank God! at last we see

There is no tribal Liberty!
No beacon lighting just our shores!
No freedom guarding but our doors!
The flame she kindled for our sires
Burns now in Europe's battle fires!
The soul that led our fathers west
Turns back to free the world's oppressed.
Allies, you have not called in vain!
We share your conflict and your pain!

"Old Glory," through new stains and rents,
Partakes of freedom's sacraments.
Across the red, shell-blasted turf
We drive the invader and his serf!
Last come, we will be last to stay —
Till right has had her crowning day!
Replenish, comrades, from our veins,
The blood the sword of despot drains,
And make our eager sacrifice
Part of that freely-rendered price
You pay to lift humanity —
You pay to make our brothers free!
See, with what proud hearts we advance
    To France.

THE GUARDS CAME THROUGH
SIR ARTHUR CONAN DOYLE

Men of the Twenty-first
  Up by the Chalk Pit Wood,
Weak with our wounds and our thirst,
  Wanting our sleep and our food,

After a day and a night—
  God, shall we ever forget!
Beaten and broke in the fight,
  But, sticking it—sticking it yet.
Trying to hold the line,
  Fainting and spent and done,
Always the thud and the whine,
  Always the yell of the Hun!
Northumberland, Lancaster, York,
  Durham and Somerset,
Fighting alone, worn to the bone,
  But sticking it—sticking it yet.

Never a message of hope!
  Never a word of cheer!
Fronting Hill 70's shell-swept slope,
  With the dull dead plain in our rear.
Always the whine of the shell,
  Always the roar of its burst,
Always the tortures of hell,
  As waiting and wincing we cursed
Our luck and the guns and the *Boche*,
  When our Corporal shouted, "Stand to!"
And I heard some one cry, "Clear the front for
    the Guards!"
  And the Guards came through.

Our throats they were parched and hot,
  But Lord, if you'd heard the cheers!
Irish and Welsh and Scot,
  Coldstream and Grenadiers.
Two brigades, if you please,
  Dressing as straight as a hem,

THE GUARDS CAME THROUGH

We — we were down on our knees,
    Praying for us and for them!
Lord, I could speak for a week,
    But how could you understand!
How should *your* cheeks be wet,
    Such feelin's don't come to *you*.
But when can me or my mates forget,
    When the Guards came through?

"Five yards left extend!"
    It passed from rank to rank.
Line after line with never a bend,
    And a touch of the London swank.
A trifle of swank and dash,
    Cool as a home parade,
Twinkle and glitter and flash,
    Flinching never a shade,
With the shrapnel right in their face
    Doing their Hyde Park stunt,
Keeping their swing at an easy pace,
    Arms at the trail, eyes front!
Man, it was great to see!
    Man, it was fine to do!
It's a cot and a hospital ward for me,
But I'll tell 'em in Blighty, wherever I be,
    How the Guards came through.

                        From the *London Times*

WORLD RECONSTRUCTION[1]
OSCAR S. STRAUS

The reconstruction of the world after this war will be our concern, but it will be urged that the Monroe Doctrine forbids us to take part in European concerns. Reading Monroe's Doctrine in the light of changed conditions, we find there a warrant, if not a duty, even in its language for our country's participation in the reconstruction of the world.

The language is: "In the wars of the European powers, in matters relating to themselves, we have never taken any part, nor does it comport with our policy to do so. *It is only when our rights are invaded or seriously menaced that we resent injuries or make preparation for our defense.*" Is it not clear that if the doctrine of might should prevail and the policy of militarism triumph, that the power of defense would be the only protection that nations would have against one another, and that the Machiavellian doctrine of the necessity of States would be the final arbiter of the rights of States? If this be true, does it not clearly become our duty, not only primarily in our own interests, but secondarily in the interests of the world, to insist upon taking part in reestablishing upon a firmer basis the safeguards of international law, without which treaties can have no value?

While "righteousness exalteth a nation," the present war gives incontrovertible proof that righteousness will not protect a nation unless all other nations are likewise

[1] From a speech delivered before the National Institute of Social Sciences on April 28, 1916.

Photo by Brown Bros.

OSCAR STRAUS

exalted by righteousness. When that time arrives we shall have reached the millenium, which from present indications is sufficiently remote to justify a search for ways and means that will serve the purpose of the world in the intervening time.

It is to be hoped that out of the extreme suffering and sacrifice that this war imposes there may arise supreme wisdom among the nations. Either there will be a new day or a darker night; all depends upon how this war will end and what bulwarks the nations will erect against future cataclysms such as we are now witnessing. In conclusion, let me repeat, America is as much concerned in the world's peace as the [other] nations at war. We must take a part in the reconstruction. Norman Angell significantly says that if we do not mix in European affairs Europe will mix in our affairs. We owe it to ourselves, to humanity and to the world to lend our best efforts and to make our fullest contribution to that reconstruction which must come.

JUDGMENT DAY
JOHN OXENHAM

The nations are in the proving;
Each day is Judgment Day;
And the peoples He finds wanting
Shall pass — by the Shadowy Way.

THE UNIVERSAL PEACE
ALFRED TENNYSON

For I dipt into the future, far as human eye could see,
Saw the Vision of the world, and all the wonder that would be:

Saw the heavens fill with commerce, argosies of magic sails,
Pilots of the purple twilight, dropping down with costly bales;

Heard the heavens fill with shouting, and there rained a ghastly dew
From the nations' airy navies grappling in the central blue;

Far along the world-wide whisper of the south-wind rushing warm,
With the standards of the peoples plunging thro' the thunder-storm;

Till the war-drum throbb'd no longer, and the battle-flags were furl'd
In the Parliament of man, the Federation of the world.

There the common sense of most shall hold a fretful realm in awe,
And the kindly earth shall slumber, lapt in universal law.

—From "*Locksley Hall*"

JOHN TIMOTHY STONE

THE YEAR BEFORE US
JOHN TIMOTHY STONE

Our nation has entered the great world strife for freedom, liberty and right, taking the same stand for the world which she took for herself in 1776, joining with the nations of the earth which stand for liberty of conscience and righteous freedom, and saying to the enemy of God and man, "Thus far shalt thou go, but no farther."

No selfish motive has inspired our nation, as voiced in the Christian message of our President: "A supreme moment of history has come. The eyes of the people have been opened and they see the hand of God is laid upon the nations. He will show them favor, I devoutly believe, only if they rise to the clear heights of his own justice and mercy."

We are to "stand fast in the faith." We are to "quit ourselves like men and be strong." We are to endure hardness as good soldiers, and with it all we are to do our part to bring to a great sinning, suffering, sickened world the meaning of those words of the angel to the shepherds: "Behold, I bring you glad tidings of great joy which shall be to all people, for unto you is born this day in the city of David a Saviour, which is Christ the Lord." The "peace, good will to men" will result.

In all this strife we are following The Master. "For the Son of Man came not to be ministered unto, but to minister, and to give His life a ransom for many." Some can minister with the sword, in destroying the usurping power of the enemy. As that enemy took the sword, so shall they perish with the sword. As the Master said to

Peter: "For all they that *take* the sword shall perish with the sword." They took it against helpless Belgium. They have advanced with it that they might dominate the world. With that sword they shall perish, as Christian soldiers minister therewith.

We must literally give our lives "a ransom for many." The Saviour of man was willing to suffer and die. We must be willing to suffer and die, if need be, for a great cause that will free the world and hasten the coming of the Prince of Peace, the Saviour of mankind. We must pray and serve, watch and fight.

There is no one great note which our nation needs at this moment more than the clear, unfaltering note that Christ is in this strife, "not to be ministered unto, but to minister, and to give His life a ransom for many."

> Crowns and thrones may perish,
> Kingdoms wax and wane,
> But the Church of Jesus constant will remain.

This letter could not come to you from my heart unless I spoke clearly my conviction, as patriot as well as pastor, in all that I believe to be the strong and stirring note of Him who shed His own blood for us, and thus took life that we might live.

Let us look forward with the joyful faith of those who are willing to experience for Him, to the fullest degree, all that He sends, believing that He is "able to do exceedingly abundantly, above all that we ask or think, even according to the power that worketh in us." May this year hold for us as a nation and as individuals, the victory of arms and faith, as right triumphs over might; and justice, mercy and peace unitedly herald the coming of a better day.

LORD, GIVE ME A PLACE

Lord, give me a place in the world's great fight,
The fight for the good and the true;
A place where the wrong outrivals the right,
And there's a soldier's work to do.

Help me to grapple some monster wrong
That baffles the good and true,
With a white-hot heart, and a tireless song,
And a far hope ever in view.

Hold fast my gaze to that gleaming height,
Lest urged by reproach or applause,
I battle more from lust of fight
Than love of a Christlike cause.

And when with earth and its strife I'm through,
Let me leave it a safer place;
With a clearer field for the good and true,
And the kingdom of love and grace.

GOD SAVE OUR SPLENDID MEN
Tune: America

God save our splendid men,
Send them safe home again
  God save our men.
Make them victorious,
Patient and chivalrous,
They are so dear to us,
  God save our men.

God keep our own dear men,
From every stain of sin,
　God keep our men.
When Satan would allure,
When tempted keep them pure
Be their protection sure —
　God keep our men.

God hold our precious men,
And love them to the end,
　God hold our men.
Held in Thine arms so strong,
To Thee they all belong,
Held safe from every wrong,
　God hold our men.

THE RED CROSS[1]

THE WORLD'S GREATEST FRATERNAL ORGANIZATION

WOODROW WILSON[1]

I have not come here to-night to review for you the work of the Red Cross. I have come here simply to say a few words to you as to what it all seems to me to mean. It means a great deal.

There are two duties with which we are face to face. The first duty is to win the war, and the second duty, that goes hand in hand with it, is to win it greatly and worthily, showing the real quality of our power not only, but the real quality of our purpose and of ourselves. Of course, the first duty, the duty that we must keep in the foreground of our thought until it is accomplished, is to win the war.

But behind all this grim purpose lies the opportunity to demonstrate not only force, which will be demonstrated to the utmost, but the opportunity to demonstrate character, and it is that opportunity that we have most conspicuously in the work of the Red Cross. Not that our men in arms do not represent our character, for they do; and it is a character which those who see and realize appreciate and admire, but their duty is the duty of force. The duty of the Red Cross is the duty of mercy and succor and friendship.

Have you formed a picture in your imagination of what this war is doing for us and for the world? In my own mind I am convinced that not a hundred years of

[1] From the speech delivered in New York May 18, 1918, at the opening of the Red Cross drive.

peace could have knitted this Nation together as this single year of war has knitted it together, and, better even than that if possible, it is knitting the world together. Look at the picture: In the center of the scene four nations engaged against the world, and at every point of vantage showing that they are seeking selfish aggrandizement; and against them twenty-three governments representing the greater part of the population of the world drawn together into a new sense of community of interest, a new sense of community of purpose, a new sense of unity of life.

The Secretary of War told me an interesting incident the other day. He said when he was in Italy a member of the Italian Government was explaining to him the many reasons why Italy felt near to the United States. He said, "If you want to try an interesting experiment go up to any one of these troop trains and ask in English how many of them have been in America, and see what happens." He tried the experiment. He went up to a troop train and he said, "How many of you boys have been in America," and he said it seemed to him as if half of them sprang up and said: "Me from San Francisco," "Me from New York—all over." There was part of the heart of America in the Italian Army—people that had been knitted to us by association, who knew us, who had lived among us, who had worked shoulder to shoulder with us, and now, friends of America, were fighting for their native Italy.

Friendship is the only cement that will ever hold the world together. And this intimate contact of the great Red Cross with the peoples who are suffering the terrors and deprivations of this war is going to be one of the

THE RED CROSS

greatest instrumentalities of friendship that the world ever knew, and the center of the heart of it all, if we sustain it properly, will be this land that we so dearly love.

My friends, a great day of duty has come, and duty finds a man's soul as no kind o work can ever find it. You can not give anything to the Government of the United States, it will not accept it. There is a law of Congress against accepting even services without pay. The only thing that the Government will accept is a loan, and duties performed; but it a great deal better to give than to lend or to pay, and your great channel for giving is the American Red Cross. Down in your hearts you can not take very much satisfaction in the last analysis in lending money to the Government of the United States, because the interest which you draw will burn your pockets. It is a commercial transaction. But when you give, something of your heart, something of your soul, something of yourself goes with the gift, particularly when it is given in such form that it never can come back by way of direct benefit to yourself. You know, there is the old cynical definition of gratitude, as "the lively expectation of favors to come." Well, there is no expectation of favors to come in this kind of giving. These things are bestowed in order that the world may be a fitter place to live in, that men may be succored, that homes may be restored, that suffering may be relieved, that the face of the earth may have the blight of destruction taken away from it, and that wherever force goes, there shall go mercy and helpfulness.

Think what we have here! We call it the American Red Cross, but it is merely a branch of a great international organization, which is not only recognized by the statutes of each of the civilized governments of the world, but is recognized by international agreement and treaty as the recognized and accepted instrumentality of mercy and succor. We are members, by being members of the American Red Cross, of a great fraternity and comradeship which extends all over the world, and this cross which these ladies bore to-day is an emblem of Christianity itself.

It fills my imagination to think of the women all over this country who are busy to-night and are busy every night and every day doing the work of the Red Cross, busy with a great eagerness to find out the most serviceable thing to do, busy with a forgetfulness of all the old frivolities of their social relationships, ready to curtail the duties of the household in order that they may contribute to this common work that all their hearts are engaged in, and in doing which their hearts become acquainted with each other. When you think of this, you realize how the people of the United States are being drawn together into a great intimate family whose heart is being used for the service of the soldiers not only, but for the service of civilians where they suffer and are lost in a maze of distresses and distractions. And you have, then, this noble picture of justice and mercy as the two servants of liberty. For only where men are free do they think the thoughts of comradeship; only where they are free do they think the thoughts of sympathy; only where they are free are they mutually helpful; only where they are free do they realize their dependence upon one another and their comradeship in a common interest and common necessity.

If you could read some of the touching dispatches

which come through official channels (for even through those channels there come voices of humanity that are infinitely pathetic); if you could catch some of those voices that speak the utter longing of oppressed and helpless peoples all over the world, to hear something like the Battle Hymn of the Republic, to hear the feet of the great hosts of Liberty coming to set them free, to set their minds free, set their lives free, set their children free — you would know what comes into the heart of those who are trying to contribute all the brains and power they have to this great enterprise of Liberty. I summon you to the comradeship. I summon you to say how much and how sincerely and how unanimously you sustain the heart of the world.

BEHIND THE GUNS

HENRY EDWARD WARNER

There are three who stand behind the guns, there are
    three who bear the load —
There is one who stands behind the three, to feel the
    stinging goad;
And one of the three is the soldier brave, and one is the
    girl who slips
So quietly in by the bed, and one is the man who builds
    the ships.
And these are the three who bear the load, and the other
    one is she
Who stays and prays, and who weeps and hopes for the
    weal of the other three —
And she is the Woman who stays and prays when the
    voice of duty calls
The Boy in Khaki, the Girl in White and the Man in the
    Overalls!

And one shall go to the battle line with a song of conquest free,
And one shall tenderly feel a pulse where the heroes sick may be,
And one shall hammer and saw and calk the ship that must ride the waves
To carry the two to their work of love, where shells blast cratered graves!
And the other one, she shall weave and weep, yet smile through her gathering tears —
For the Mother-love and the Mother-pride shall conquer her Mother-tears;
And Three and One, they shall batter down fair Liberty's prison walls —
The Boy in Khaki, the Girl in White, and the Man in the Overalls!

THE RED CROSS SPIRIT SPEAKS
JOHN H. FINLEY

Wherever war, with its red woes,
Or flood, or fire, or famine goes,
   There, too, go I;
If earth in any quarter quakes
Or pestilence its ravage makes,
   Thither I fly.

I go wherever men may dare,
I go wherever woman's care
   And love can live,
Wherever strength and skill can bring
Surcease to human suffering,
   Or solace give.

I helped upon Haldora's shore;
With Hospitaller Knights I bore
    The first red cross;
I was the Lady of the Lamp;
I saw in Solferino's camp
    The crimson loss.

I am your pennies and your pounds;
I am your bodies on their rounds
    Of pain afar;
I am *you*, doing what you would
If you were only where you could —
    Your avatar.

The cross which on my arm I wear,
The flag which o'er my breast I bear,
    Is but the sign
Of what you'd sacrifice for him
Who suffers on the hellish rim
    Of war's red line.

GREY KNITTING
KATHERINE HALE

Something sings gently through the din of battle,
Something spreads very softly rim on rim
And every soldier hears, at times, a murmur
Tender, incessant — dim.

A tiny click of little wooden needles,
Elfin amid the gianthood of war;
Whispers of women, tireless and patient,
Who weave the web afar.

Whispers of women, tireless and patient —
'Foolish, inadequate!' we hear you say;
'Grey wool on fields of hell is out of fashion,'
And yet we weave the web from day to day.

And so each soldier, laughing, fighting — dying
Under the alien skies, in his great hour,
May listen, in death's prescience all-enfolding,
And hear a fairy sound bloom like a flower —

I like to think that soldiers, gaily dying
For the white Christ on fields with shame sown deep
May hear the tender sound of women's needles,
As they fall fast asleep.

NEWTON D. BAKER

THE TASK OF THE RED CROSS
NEWTON D. BAKER

The human race is a waif left to die unless we, trustees, accept the task of rescuing it.

I suppose there has not been, since the very early times in human history, a war in which slaughter was so casual as it is in this.

I speak of its casual character because for a great many hundred years we have been progressing in the direction of limiting the horrors of war to the combatants, and that in this Twentieth Century we should revert to the casual slaughter of children, to the improvident slaughter of women, to the theory of warfare by the extermination of peoples, and to the use of weapons of war like starvation and disease is an unthinkable reversion to barbarous type which it was the hope of the intelligent that the world had outgrown.

We are entering the war in the firm belief and purpose of ending it in a victory for right — and we have not the slightest intention of stopping until that victory is achieved.

Mad as the world seems to be, some day there will be reëstablished on this stricken planet a peace which will be just and wise and permanent, just in proportion as America pours out her spiritual resources in the waging of the war from now on and is heard at the conference table to challenge the attention of mankind to the beauty of righteousness among nations. But in the meantime, as the armies which are being called are trained and are led to battle, all along the national wayside of every nation in the world, still crouch the terrified and trampled figures of the children of mankind, disowned, starving, and dying. There is no limit to it, and I shall not undertake to harrow your feelings — in fact, I am not certain that I could command myself to repeat the heart-rendering messages of intimate letters which I have seen with in the last day or two about Roumania. But the call is limitless and it is to be made known to the hearts of the people of the United States, and we are going to endeavor to respond to this cry of distress.

The Red Cross of the United States of America has set itself the great task of raising for, one might say, cosmic philanthropy, a sum equal to the destruction which the war entails in a day.

The response which we ought to make ought to be limited only by the extent to which our sympathy, enlightened by knowledge and stirred by imagination and then understepping rather than overstepping the mark, will enable us to make sacrifices for the greatest need the world has ever known.

YOUTH SPEAKS TO YOUTH[1]

From an American Student to the
Girls of France

    To you, there in the van,
    Thronging hundreds of France,
    Who through dark mists march to the light,
    Forging a way toward the new dawning —

---

[1] These messages were really sent across the Atlantic Ocean by an American and a French girl.

We come, we, the recruits,
Adding strength to your strength —
Youth to your youth —
That when the mists clear and dawn lightens
 the wreck of the world,
We may join in rebuilding.

A French Girl Replies

It was only a little river, almost a brook; it was called the Yser. One could talk from one side to the other without raising one's voice, and the birds could fly over it with one sweep of their wings. And on the two banks there were millions of men, the one turned toward the other, eye to eye. But the distance which separated them was greater than the stars in the sky; it was the distance which separates right from injustice.

The ocean is so great that the sea gulls do not dare to cross it. During seven days and seven nights the great steamships of America, going at full speed, drive through the deep waters before the lighthouses of France come into view; but from one side to the other hearts are touching.

THE RED CROSS NURSES

THOMAS L. MASSON

Out where the line of battle cleaves
The horizon of woe
And sightless warriors clutch the leaves
The Red Cross nurses go.
In where the cots of agony
Mark death's unmeasured tide —

Bear up the battle's harvestry —
The Red Cross nurses glide.

Look! Where the hell of steel has torn
Its way through slumbering earth
The orphaned urchins kneel forlorn
And wonder at their birth.
Until, above them, calm and wise
With smile and guiding hand,
God looking through their gentle eyes
The Red Cross nurses stand.

WITH THE AMERICAN RED CROSS IN FRANCE[1]
HENRY P. DAVISON

I never have known the morale as high all along the line and back of the line as it is today. And I believe the American Red Cross is more responsible for this than any other single agency.

The purpose of the fight behind the line is to break down the morale of the civilian population to such a point that they will importune their governments for peace. It is the most dastardly, unrighteous, cruel, devilish plan which could be conceived. It is based upon the theory that the killing of four children out of five will induce the mother to implore her government to have the war stopped that her fifth child may live. It is carried on from the British Channel to the Swiss border and from the Swiss border to the Adriatic. It has resulted in the murder and maiming of thousands of women and children and the driving of hundreds of thousands from their homes.

I wish I could give you a picture of one of those nights. We went into a town of about fifty thousand about six o'clock one evening. About half past seven we started over to the Red Cross canteen. As we went into the main street, I noticed a concourse of people all going in one direction. After walking along with them three or four minutes I said, "What is going on, what is this?" They said these people were moving out for the night to the caves.

---
[1] From a speech delivered in Chicago, May 23, 1918.

There were old men, women, and children. For instance, one would see a mother walking with a girl of fourteen, a girl of twelve, a child of seven, and a child of one in her arms, carrying a small mattress, pillows, any coverlets whatever, that they might have a night not of sleep, but of security in a cave a mile and a half outside the town. That was my first view of people seeking refuge from the aerial bombardment.

I went over to our canteen. It had been an old warehouse and had been fixed up by camouflage artists. In the main room were tables where soldiers could have meals. Back of that was a large room with cots for the soldiers to sleep. Next to that was a room where the soldiers could take off their clothes and, while they were bathing, the clothes could be fumigated.

I walked around in the crowd and in the cashier's office one of the girls stepped up and pulled down the window. I asked, "What has happened?" She said, "The raid is coming, we must get to a place of safety." I said, "You come with me." She said, "O, never. Do you think that I, as head of this canteen, could leave this building while there is a French soldier in it? Do you think an American woman could run from a bomb in the presence of a Frenchman?"

Well, after a bit we went to the *abri*, built of reinforced concrete, with sandbags over the top. It would hold, perhaps, one hundred people. The signal that the raid was over was sounded at half past ten and we went out. I asked, "Are you going home?" They said, "What, going home? We are open twenty-three hours a day. We close only between seven and eight in the morning that the place may be cleaned." They went back and I went to the hotel.

We retired and were awakened about one o'clock by the breaking in of our windows. That indicated another air raid was on — and so, through the night, that town was bombarded. In the morning we saw the people going about more or less in their usual demeanor. Of course, they were paralyzed with fear, but there wasn't any sign of weakening.

Three days later that town was evacuated by its civilian population. The soldiers of the French army remained, and you may know that the eighteen American women are still there running the canteen. They will continue to do so as long as there are any soldiers there.

THE FEET OF THE CHILDREN
NORA ARCHIBALD SMITH

In far Arabia they tell the tale—
A wondrous tale, e'en in the home of wonders—
Of that great magic-worker, whose fine ear,
Held to the ground in any desert's core,
Yet could detect on Bagdad's stony ways
The pattering of little children's feet
And hear their laughter and their frolicking.

A wondrous tale indeed; and yet today,
In this new land that never held enchantment,
Day after day the miracle is wrought again.
No woman's ear that is not pressed to earth
Each day she wakens, while with anguished heart
She hears the echoing of children's feet,
Bare feet and wayworn, in the wilderness.

Oh, little feet in Flanders and in France;
Strayed feet in Belgium's vast orphanage;
Feet that have never sinned and yet must bleed
In Germany's stark homes and swollen graveyards
Small feet of woe in Russia's cruel snows;
Armenian feet and Polish, Serb and Austrian,
We hear your terror in your pattering.

We may not bear the load of anguish more;
Each step falls like a weight of iron down.
We feel the frozen touch, the icy chill,
Of flesh that life may never warm again.
Oh, feet unsheltered from the wintry blast,
Dear feet that never walked uncompanied,
God send you safely into paradise!

WHEN THE BOYS COME HOME
JOHN HAY

There's a happy time coming,
  When the boys come home.
There's a glorious day coming,
  When the boys come home.
We will end the dreadful story
Of this treason dark and gory
In a sunburst of glory,
  When the boys come home.

The day will seem brighter
  When the boys come home,
For our hearts will be lighter
  When the boys come home.
Wives and sweethearts will press them
In their arms and caress them,
And pray God to bless them,
  When the boys come home.

The thinned ranks will be proudest
  When the boys come home,
And their cheer will ring the loudest
  When the boys come home.
The full ranks will be shattered,
And the bright arms will be battered,
And the battle-standards tattered,
  When the boys come home.

Their bayonets may be rusty,
  When the boys come home,
And their uniforms dusty,
  When the boys come home.
But all shall see the traces
Of battle's royal graces,
In the brown and bearded faces,
  When the boys come home.

Our love shall go to meet them,
  When the boys come home,
To bless them and to greet them,
  When the boys come home;
And the fame of their endeavor
Time and change shall not dissever
From the nation's heart forever,
  When the boys come home.

www.ingramcontent.com/pod-product-compliance
Lightning Source LLC
Chambersburg PA
CBHW011958150426
43201CB00018B/2326